To Johnny

YOU MAY AS WELL
LAUGH
AS
CRY

by
Emma Mae Robbins

National Library of Canada Cataloguing in Publication Data

Robbins, Emma Mae
      You May As Well Laugh As Cry

ISBN 0-9737441-0-3

Printed and bound in Canada

Published in Canada by
Murder Bay Publishers Ltd.
251 Beecher Bay Road
Sooke, B.C.
Canada
V0S 1N0

INTRODUCTION

Choosing the right title for a book can be the most challenging and difficult part of the entire process. Over the course of putting together this book, I had jotted down several titles that I thought might be suitable. However, none of them seemed to be the "fit" I was looking for.

As so often happens, we find what we are searching for when we have actually forgotten the search. One drizzly afternoon in late November, I started thinking about a last visit with my cousin, Travis, who lived in New Brunswick. His wife, Melva, was in the advanced stages of Alzheimer's. We had all gone out to dinner at a local restaurant and, during the whole evening, Melva had not spoken one word. It was sad to see someone who had always been so vibrant, creative, and witty, reduced to merely a silent presence at our table.

Before leaving the restaurant, Melva started for the washroom and I followed along. As we were both washing up at the sinks, she looked into the long mirror over the counter and ran her fingers carelessly through her short grey hair. I was startled to hear her say, "I look like the wreck of the Hesperus." It was an expression we had both used while growing up, taken from a poem we had learned in grade five. I looked into her eyes and, all of a sudden, we both started to laugh. Melva gave her hair another cursory brush and then she remarked in that dry, measured tone that had been so characteristically hers, "You may as well laugh as cry."

The next instant, she returned to her silent, secret place, but for that one brief moment we had shared something human and wonderful again. I never forgot those seven words, however, and as I recalled the incident on that dreary November afternoon, I found the title to this book.

As in Melva's situation, there are so many things in life beyond our control - everyday incidents and events that may leave us angry, frustrated, disillusioned - rude and inconsiderate people, relationship problems, challenges of raising a family, driving in traffic, taxes, rising energy prices, new technologies, growing older.

To be able to look at these through the lighter lens of humour helps to make them, if not lesser, than at least manageable. My hope is that this book will make you laugh when you want to cry - even when you may feel like the wreck of the Hesperus.

The breakers were right beneath her bows,
She drifted a dreary wreck,
And a whooping billow swept the crew
Like icicles from her deck.
She struck where the white and fleecy waves
Looked soft as carded wool,
But the cruel rocks, they gored her side
Like the horns of an angry bull.
Her rattling shrouds, all sheathed in ice,
With the masts went by the board;
Like a vessel of glass, she stove and sank,
Ho! ho! the breakers roared!

From *The Wreck of the Hesperus*
by Henry Wadsworth Longfellow

SEARCHING FOR SIGMUND FREUD AND STEPHEN LEACOCK AT THE SAVEASY

I hate supermarkets. Maybe it's because I have spent nearly two thousand hours of my life wandering up and down their aisles, comparing grams and millilitres, seeking out the lowest price on everything from soup to nachos, in an attempt to get what Sprint Canada once promised: "the most for the least." I think, though, for someone like Sigmund Freud, supermarkets would have been a goldmine for psychological research, because there is no place that better reveals the folly of human behaviour, unless it is a little league hockey game.

Take the express checkout, the gathering place for the "rule pushers" of society. If the sign says "9 items or less," they will have at least a dozen. Last week, as I was approaching the express till with 20 grams of sesame seeds, a woman edged in front of me with a cart that looked like a hanging basket. She started unloading her booty, consisting of twenty-four cans of clamato juice, ten boxes of cereal and a case of cream of mushroom soup. When the young clerk pointed to the "9 items or less" sign, the woman became indignant, claiming that in reality she only had **THREE** things: juice, cereal and soup. A question of semantics, I guess, or there's always the possibility she is a lawyer, skilled in the art of arguing technicalities and pointing out distinctions without a difference.

Actually, standing in the tabloid corridor that leads to the checkout can be an enlightening and entertaining experience. Freud would have revelled in it, particularly the sexual undertones. There was Julia Roberts with all her teeth in and Pamela Anderson with all her breasts out, and a picture of an alien infant born to a seventy-five year old woman in Albuquerque. It looked as if someone had photographed one of the Teletubbies and superimposed it over a picture of Dr. Ruth.

I've long believed supermarkets should have a CCF checkout. No, I'm not referring to a defunct Canadian political party. I mean a checkout strictly to handle three things: cigarettes, coupons and flowers. Have you ever stood in line behind a shopper who, after their groceries are tallied up, asks for a package of cigarettes? What follows closely resembles a national inquiry: Plain or Filter tip? Extra light or full flavour? Extra long or full figure? Liberal or Conservative? Subsequently, after the customer has asked for Rotgut extra long full flavour Liberal, the clerk disappears with a set of keys for the next twenty minutes, only to return and announce that they are all out of Rotgut extra long full flavour Liberal cigarettes. And so begins a whole new process of substitution.

Then there are those coupons. I'm sure it was coupons that were responsible for that wartime expression SNAFU. Either the customer has picked up a Hyland brand of soup instead of the Lowland variety designated on the face of the coupon, or the coupon states it is good for two packages of Loveadog cat foot and the shopper is trying to apply it to a caseload. Either way, you know as you stand there, trapped in the checkout line, that by the time you get through with your own groceries your pre-schooler will be old enough to vote.

I love flowers as much as the next person. But flowers in a supermarket line-up cause problems. You see, a bouquet of flowers has to be wrapped, and for some reason this wrapping process seems to open up previously non-existent lines of communication between the wrapper and the wrappee. A lengthy dialogue ensues as to who the flowers are for and what the occasion is and what a lovely evening it is going to be and will there be wine and candles too? Experts will tell you that most panic attacks occur in supermarket line-ups.

If the express checkout deviants and the tabloid sleaze didn't provide Sigmund with enough material for his supermarket treatise, he may well have completed his research at the bulk food section. This is where theft is committed, every single day. I don't mean a tiny nibble here and there; I'm talking about ingesting the equivalent of a three-course meal. One day I watched a middle-aged couple engaging in a bulk food buffet, eating their way from one bin to another until finally a young store worker politely brought the matter to their attention. Were they ashamed? Did they show remorse? Not on your life. They let him know they were having guests that evening and needed to know if the cashew nuts were fresh because, by golly, if they weren't fresh enough for *them* they certainly wouldn't think of feeding them to their *guests*.

Their response reminded me of a story I read in high school, "The Sinking of the Mariposa Belle" by Stephen Leacock. As the Mariposa Belle is going down in six feet of water, the cry "Women and children first!" is raised, because, according to Leacock, "what was the sense, if it should turn out that the boat wouldn't even hold women and children, of trying to jam a lot of heavy men into it?"

But I digress. I had been talking about nuts in the supermarket. By now the purloining pair had quit sampling the cashews. It's hard to eat nuts when your mouth is full of gummy bears.

I'd like to propose some changes to the supermarket industry. To deter food samplers, scanners could be mounted above the bins to detect when a shopper attempts to taste the wares. As soon as he or she puts something in their mouth a voice booms "She did it!" or "He did it!" Within two months food prices would drop due to the decrease in shoplifting. And as for the "rule pushers" at the express counter, a guillotine affair, which drops after the ninth item, should do the trick. It's not everyone who can handle split peas, sliced almonds and chopped liver with broken fingers.

GREEN JELLY BEANS ARE BETTER THAN TURKEYS

Where was the Green Jelly Bean Game when I needed it? Surely you've heard of it, that "red herring" exercise developed by the Canadian Navy to keep the kids busy when Mom or Dad return from a long absence at sea. The adults hide forty-nine green jelly beans amidst the blades of lawn grass and then send the children out to find fifty. While the kids are looking for that fiftieth jelly bean, Mom and Dad become "re-acquainted." If the Green Jelly Bean Game is not the sole property of the Department of National Defence, I would like to see it made available to all parents facing the most daunting challenge of child rearing - hosting a birthday party.

Unfortunately, I heard about the game too late. It was over 30 years ago that I held my first birthday party for our son who was just turning six. I sent invitations to five of the little neighbourhood rascals, one of whom was Daryl, "the one most likely to demolish your home."

We spent an hour playing "Pin the Nose On The Clown" (a clever re-creation of the donkey-tail version), "Blind Man's Bluff" and "Hot Potato," using a stale dinner roll. Then the little monsters gathered around the dining room table under a cascade of streamers and balloons where they devoured a dozen hot dogs, a gallon of ice cream and a four-pound cake decorated with little yellow airplanes sitting on a chocolate runway illuminated by six blue candles.

When the party blissfully ended, I handed each of the boys a treat bag. Daryl immediately unfolded the top of the bag, peered inside and said, "Is this all we get?" I'm certain it was Daryl who originated the expression, "Is that all there is?"

If only I had known about the Green Jelly Bean Game then, Daryl might have grown up to be an archaeologist instead of a thief. And it would have become an integral part of my life in subsequent years as my family increased in number, much more effective than that silly scavenger hunt I organized for my daughter's 7th birthday. You see, the problem was, I didn't use my imagination. By then we were living on a little farm and I should have realized that things like "a piece of straw, a white rock," and "a feather," were standard fare for the country, good for about 45 seconds of a three-hour birthday party. If I'd been smart I'd have asked them to find "a bowling ball, a Macdonald's Happy Meal wrapper" or "a hood ornament for a 1950 Chevy."

Or I could have scattered 49 green jelly beans in the hay field, giving me time to pour a glass of cabernet, call my sister in Moose Jaw, and finish the last chapter of *War and Peace*.

Such was not the case. Within three minutes I was met by half a dozen seven-year-olds holding a piece of straw, a white rock and a feather, and every child was bursting with enough potential energy to launch a scud missile. In desperation, I realized I had to devise another game plan. I resorted to turkeys.

That morning we had picked up a dozen baby turkeys at the hatchery. They were still in the delivery box in the mud room and they proved to be a fascination for my little party animals, particularly the ones who lived in town. For the next two hours they adopted the chicks like tamagotchi pets. The turkeys went camping with Barbie and Ken, occupied thrones in the Fisher Price castle, and took over the barn reserved for My Little Ponies.

When the party ended and it was time to take the little girls home, I passed out the treat bags. At that moment my husband decided to add something extra to the birthday loot. He gave each child a farm fresh egg. It started out well enough, with each girl carefully, almost reverently, placing the egg inside the pocket of her coat. However, on the way home, as Ashley jumped on Allison in the back of the van, as Teresa scrunched too close to Jenna, and as Jennifer wadded up her coat to use as a pillow, I realized that another party at our house might be a distinct impossibility.

Yes, the Green Jelly Bean Game would have been a better idea. Jelly beans are definitely cleaner, firmer and more durable than free range eggs.

FROM HOUSEKEEPER TO MOUSEKEEPER

I see where scientists have produced a "Mighty Mouse," not the one we watched on Saturday morning cartoons a generation ago, but a "super-mouse," produced by inhibiting the blocking action of myostatin, a growth factor in the mouse's DNA. Super Bowl contenders pay attention! Here, at last, a way to inhibit the blocking action of the Green Bay Packers.

After living on a ranch in Alberta I wonder who needs larger mice. When my father-in-law moved west from Ontario and someone boasted to him about the fact that Alberta had no rats he said, "Maybe not, but they sure make up for it in mice." And when my mother moved to Alberta and someone told her the "no rat" story she simply said, "No wonder. No rat would stay here. It's too cold."

The Latin description of the house mouse sounds like a preamble for the installation of a lodge member: *Mus musculus* of the *Order Rodentia.*" When it comes to a mouse invasion of your residence, however, there *is* no order. According to the *Encyclopaedia Britannica*, "Mice are common and indigenous to almost every land area." Well, no wonder. The mating habits of mice remind one of a revolving door. One little *mus musculus* can mate three months after birth, producing up to a dozen more little *rodentias* which will mate three months after their birth, and so on and so on. The encyclopaedia further states that "minor infestations of mice can be handled by trapping." This is a delusion. The trap line I operated in that little cedar-lined ranch house could have covered the length of the Canada-U.S. border.

One day my children found a nest of six baby mice in the granary. They decided to "raise" them in the empty aquarium where

11

the tropical fish had expired. Their tiny adoptees had to be fed with a doll's nursing bottle.

"Aren't they cute, Mom?" they squealed, (my children, I mean, not the mice). I had to admit, each time those baby rodents lay on their backs and placed their tiny, human-like paws around the neck of the bottle, they *did* look cute.

However, there is a universal truth somewhere out there in the cosmos that states, "Children will tire of their pets." There must also be an unwritten commandment in the same cosmos that says, "Mothers, thou shalt pick up the slack." I couldn't just let these little creatures starve to death. They grew faster than house prices in Vancouver. In fact, I experienced the empty nest syndrome sooner than I figured - the morning I found the empty aquarium. They had escaped. All six of them. When I found their droppings on the cupboard shelf beside the nibbled hole in the *Miniwheats* box, I decided they were no longer cute. I will refrain from telling "the rest of the story." Content yourself with the knowledge that they are now peacefully munching in "that great cheese factory in the sky," somewhere out there with Timothy Leary. In fact, if you look to the north some fine, starry night, you just might see them blinking away under Cassiopeia's Chair.

Enough about my personal experience with mice. It's back to science. Apparently the idea behind the inhibition of myostatin is the eventual production of larger cattle and chickens. After having the experience of staring down a 2,000 pound Charolais bull that had escaped from its corral, I have no desire to see a larger bovine, but I have to admit, it would be hard to turn down a five-pound chicken breast.

- *At present I operate a trap line for computer mice.*

THE AWESOME POWER
IN A SELF-SEALING POT

I always give my husband fishing lures for his birthday. Last year, however, I decided to try something different. Not only does my husband love to fish; he loves to cook his catch. Our pots and pans were starting to look as though they had been excavated from an ancient burial chamber, so I decided to surprise him with some shiny new ones. For $300.00 I bought him a nine-piece set of stainless steel cookware with a lifetime guarantee. I wrapped them in paper covered with pictures of fish and made a card that said, "For cod's sake, cook your heart out!"

He was delighted. I almost envied him banging around the kitchen with such fine cooking utensils. Not enough, though, to beg my way back to the stove. One day he made a pot of fish chowder from the codfish he had caught with his favourite lure. It was a gourmet's dream - creamy white broth with chunks of fresh cod and potatoes, grated carrots, chopped onions and God knows what else a dreamy gourmet puts into a chowder.

When it was finished he put it out on the balcony to cool. A big mistake. You see, neither of us realized these were "self-sealing" pots. When he retrieved the pot of chowder a few hours later, the top was stuck tighter than a two-year-old to a soother.

I tried to pry it off with an assortment of devices - a knife, a nail file, a bottle opener - with no success. My husband resorted to his toolbox. But when the chisels and the crowbar didn't budge the lid, we knew we had a real problem on our hands. Suddenly I knew the meaning of "lifetime guarantee." Anything sealed inside those pots was guaranteed to be there for a lifetime.

The next day I took the stubborn pot to our local locksmith but he said he only worked on objects that have keyholes.

I discussed the problem with my doctor. "Perhaps you could perform surgery on it?" I proposed. The doctor advised that he only operated on bone and tissue, not metal. He suggested a plumber.

"The only solution is a welding torch," said the plumber, solemnly. "Do you really want to take such an extreme measure?" No, I assured him, at this point I only wanted to *open* the pot, not melt it.

Several months later I flew to Alberta to visit my daughter. Since my son-in-law is a champion roper, I threw the pot into my suitcase. Maybe he would be able to help me. I can tell you he tried his very best. After roping the knob on the lid of that pot and dragging it all over the ranch with no success, he offered to shoot the cover off with his .22 rifle. I declined.

In desperation I turned to Darby, an ex con. Darby had just finished serving six days of a six-year sentence for a string of break and enters. He asked to keep the pot overnight since he preferred to work in the dark. The next day he brought it back, unopened. Darby said in his entire crime career he had never come across anything he couldn't break into. The pot had spoiled his record. He advised me to see a lawyer.

I made an appointment with Les Fleece, Barrister and Solicitor, who dealt exclusively in difficult cases. He studied the pot for a long time and then he asked, "Was there *mens rea?*"

"No," I said, "there's just my man's pot." He explained that *mens rea* is a Latin term used by the legal profession to designate intent. If I had *intended* to seal the pot, he would not be able to take the case. I assured him that intent to seal was the furthest thing from my mind.

Three days later Mr. Fleece called me into his office. The pot was open. The chowder was stale dated but still edible. As I wrote a cheque for his $300.00 fee, I asked him how he had managed to pull it off. After a lot of "whereases, heretofores" and "up-yourses," he admitted he had found just the *tiniest* loophole.

I took the pot home and cleaned it up. Then I filled it with fishing lures and wrapped it in paper covered with fish pictures. I'm saving it for my husband's next birthday.

FASHION CONSPIRACY

Stuart Wilde in his book *Affirmations*, talks about "The Circle," a group of 2000 families "dedicated to the control of mankind." I think I know one area where this Circle operates: women's clothing fashions.

Perhaps the greatest injustice done to North American women is the creation of the tracksuit. As soon as you put one on you immediately gain twenty pounds. And those colours! All funereal. Who said black is slimming? Not in a tracksuit, it isn't. Even the name is a misnomer. The word "track" implies a sinewy, sweat-drenched figure racing with the speed of a cheetah. Now tell me, have you ever seen anyone dressed in a tracksuit who was actually ***running***? Back in 1759, at the conclusion of the Battle of the Plains of Abraham, there is a verbal exchange between General Wolfe and one of his officers. As Wolfe lies dying on the battlefield, the officer says, "See how they run, sir." Wolfe's lips form around his last words, "Who runs?" The soldier answers proudly, "The French, Sir." I'll bet my last bagel that not one soldier, English or French, was wearing a tracksuit.

It appears that fashion designers have contrived to make women look as unattractive as possible. For years they tried to deny the existence of legs. I was at a party recently and a friend showed up in a lovely two-piece knit dress. She appeared a little self-conscious, finally confiding, "I haven't worn a skirt for so long I feel like a transvestite." Think of it. When was the last time you saw an actual leg or even a "well-turned ankle?" I recall a conversation with a psychiatrist at a social occasion several years ago. Having imbibed enough to share his secret thoughts, he leaned over and whispered, "I haven't seen a woman's legs in so long I think I might go crazy!"

Sometimes I wonder if some of the women's fashions were inspired by the animal kingdom. Perhaps some Italian designer by the name of Lucci Lunni (pronounced Looney) was sitting beside a swamp one day when he became enamoured by the legs of a stork. The result? Leggings. Unfortunately, because most of us have thighs like a setting hen, the stork look didn't work and Lunni had to come up with something to cover the leggings, He created oversized t-shirts that made us all look eight months pregnant.

These fashion people weren't content to stop at women's legs. They went all the way, creating footwear designed to lame and maim - those with heels like post malls and heavy enough to anchor a Great Lakes freighter. And then we have the four-inch stiletto heels. Did you ever watch a woman trying to manoeuvre in either of these? Designers might claim they have raised us to a new level. It is now possible for women to wash second storey windows and drywall ceilings. It is just not possible to walk. Then we have those sandals that came out of a discount store for baby susquatches. You can put a pair of those on and increase your shoe size by 200%. And you can increase your *weight* by that much just by slipping into a pair of women's boots. A single boot exceeds the carry-on limit for aircraft.

Of course, the boots may have advantages. They would be invaluable on Roll Back day at Walmart when you are jostling other shoppers for a cartload of toilet tissue and an armload of paper towels. And they should be required equipment for dancing courses. That way if you end up with a partner who has two left feet you will have two feet left.

I haven't mentioned the bare midriff look inspired by a certain rock singer. All I can say is, the day this one becomes obsolete, we will all be able to lift up our eyes unto the hills once again without being assaulted by hanging and bulging body parts everywhere we look.

What I wonder is, what will become of all this "stuff" when another fashion craze takes its place? I say give the clothing back to the animal kingdom where it belongs - the track suits to the hippos who don't run, the leggings to arthritic storks to keep them warm and the t-shirts to post-natal penguins with the logo, "Have you pecked your chick today?" The shoes? They may well be classed as restricted weapons whereupon they will be seized by the RCMP. As for the boots, they would make great ballast for ships.

But the greatest benefit is this. The minute we cast off our track suits we will immediately drop twenty pounds, which means we won't have to run when we wear them, which we never did anyway, but at least the guilt will be gone.

YOU CAN BET ON A POKEMON BUT NOT ON A TURNIP HORSE

Whatever happened to *Sing and Snore Ernie*? Can you recall how many years ago it was that parents scrambled to department stores to duke it out with other parents over a dumpy little doll that could sing and snore? And the season before that, didn't those same parents put a hammerlock on each other in their struggle for a *Tickle Me Elmo*? One year the playmate responsible for guerrilla warfare among parents was a furry little character with a mechanical voice that made you want to commit Furbicide. Eventually, even Furby was replaced by something called the Pokemon phenomenon, consisting of games, cards, dolls, and even a movie.

All this Christmas toy hype takes me back to the early 80s when little girls threatened to self-destruct if they didn't own a Cabbage Patch doll. In early October of that particular year I asked Doris, the owner of the local hardware store, when they would be stocking some Cabbage Patch dolls. Doris advised the dolls were on "back order," whatever that meant. I put my name down on her list and cast my future as a parent to the gods of toyland. Two weeks later I received a call. It was Doris. Sounding like an undercover CIA agent, she whispered into the receiver.

"They're here - the Cabbage Patch dolls! You'd better get down here, NOW!"

I left my bread dough in mid-rise and raced down to the store. Doris ushered me into the back room where three rows of Cabbage Patch dolls lined the wall, waiting for adoption. There were several other mothers in the room, most of whom I knew well, but at that moment they all became adversaries. I spotted a girl doll with a bright yellow dress and long brown braids, the exact one my daughter had her heart set on. Snatching it up, I muttered to Doris, "Put it on my account," and slipped out the door. I felt as if I were a member of some underground movement, spiriting Cabbage Patch dolls out of back rooms and into the bottom of my closet.

There was another year, too, when Wonder Woman was queen of the air waves, spinning like a spider on amphetamines and knocking the daylights out of every thug and gangster within her energy field. Naturally, just before Christmas, a Wonder Woman doll appeared, whirling and whacking its way across the t.v. screen like its human prototype. My daughter was sucked in. On Christmas morning, as she tore open the wrapping to reveal Wonder Woman in her skimpy red outfit, she squealed in glee. The next moment, however, her little face turned into a sidehill slump.

"Hey!" she exclaimed. "She doesn't SPIN!"

She has never forgotten the Wonder Woman doll, nor the lesson she learned that Christmas about the fallacy of television advertising.

I sometimes wonder what my grandfather would have said about all this toy hysteria, he, who, as a little boy, whittled toy horses out of turnips.

"They were o.k. until they dried up," he would laugh as he told the story.

The year *Sing and Snore Ernie* was hot, I had a discussion with a young woman who was working on her fourth year of marriage.

"I think I'll buy an Ernie for myself," she said. "He's cute and he doesn't make gross noises in bed. And another thing, when he wakes up he says something *nice*."

Toys that promise the idyllic are nothing new. Fifty years ago Tennessee Ernie Ford sang a song entitled, "Automatic Woman."

"I want an automatic woman with a hydromatic drive
To kiss me every evening when I come home at five.
I'll turn the switch to stop her when she starts to scream and moan
And when I want some lovin', just turn the button on."

Imagine if television had been king in those days. The number one item on the Christmas list of every North American male would have been: automatic woman.

Automation was undoubtedly the key to Pokemon's success and it has been claimed that the Pokemon cards enhance memory. Anything that will help me remember five items on a shopping list or my mother's postal code is definitely worth investigating. But first I plan to dig out my son's old hockey equipment, particularly the shin pads and elbow pads. When you wade into the middle of a Pokemon phenomenon you need to be able to spin and whack - like Wonder Woman.

POLITICIANS ARE ADVISED TO STAY AWAY FROM COOKIES

I know none of my children, and certainly not any of yours, would ever admit to stealing cookies. But in our house cookies just seemed to disappear, into thin air, and the culprit was always the same person:

"Who took the cookies out of the freezer?"

"Not me."

"Who emptied the cookie jar?"

"Not me."

"Who ate the cookies in Daddy's lunch?"

"Not me."

Heaven knows, I did my best to insure an endless supply of cookies. I finally gave up hiding them in the bottom of the freezer. They were far too accessible and posed too much of a temptation. I found other places: the tool box under the basement stairs, the sock drawer in the bottom of the antique dresser, the container marked "dried turnip chips" on the top shelf of the pantry. To no avail. Every time I went to retrieve the cookies I had so carefully stashed, I was greeted by an empty container.

A few years ago, however, I stumbled upon the truth. I read in the newspaper that it is possible to store cookies on your computer. The writer of the article used a lot of cyber-language but I think I figured out what she was trying to say. Cookies, she maintained, can be downloaded into your hard drive while you are browsing certain web sites, sometimes without your knowledge.

For example, suppose you are a noted politician with a difficult portfolio and you are continually being harassed by some segment of the population because you can't seem to please all of the people all of the time. One night, while working late at the office, you sit down at your computer and log on to the Internet. Your intention is to find a web site that deals with "Exit Strategies" in the hope that it will provide tips on how to avoid all those hecklers and protesters. For a few minutes you scroll through information about tunnels, back doors, decoys, red herrings and camouflaged vehicles. But then - completely by accident of course - you wander into a web site labelled "Exotic Sex". Suddenly your screen is filled with a rapid succession of virtually nude females, bursting with enough silicone to seal every window in the Parliament buildings, and all of them mouthing words you have never heard, even from protesters and hecklers.

Immediately upon discovering your error, (give or take an hour) you return to your search for "Exit Strategies" as was your original intention. However, the fact is, that while you were being titillated at the "Exotic Sex" web site, little bits of information about that particular site were being quietly and clandestinely downloaded into your computer. It is a known fact that cookies are bad for your health. Read on.

Now suppose - just suppose - that some member from the opposing party gains access to your computer. Stranger things have happened. Remember Watergate? Suddenly in the next day's newspaper, there it is, spattered across the front page in big bold letters: "Minister of Difficult Portfolios Caught in Exotic Sex Web." All the sleazy, dark corners of your mind have been exposed. You are like a cockroach under a halogen bulb. The proof is not in the pudding. It is in the cookie. Because of you, the country is faced with a lengthy, expensive national inquiry followed by a Royal Commission. You, of all people, will go down in history as the creator of the Great Canadian Cookiegate Scandal and the only surfing you will do from now on is over the classified pages under the "Employment Wanted" column. At least when you complete an application for another job and you come to the question "Reason for leaving last place of employment," you will have something to fill the blank. "Too many cookies."

But as I said at the beginning of this article, all of this is just cyber-talk, something to fill the "Business" pages of the newspaper. There is a far greater truth to be revealed here. Those cookies that went missing from my household didn't disappear into thin air. They have been floating around in cyberspace all this time. "Not Me," is innocent after all.

Oh, to have been computer-literate in those days! After a session of baking I could have simply stored my wares in the hard drive, encoded a password known only to me, (something like "dried turnip chips") and tuned into the next episode of *Thorn Birds*, knowing my cookies were safe. Alas! Sometimes progress arrives too late.

* I am still looking for a dozen chocolate chip cookies that disappeared in May of 1986. If found, please contact www.emmamae'scookies.com.

CELL PHONES ARE FOR THOSE WHO ARE MENTALLY INCARCERATED

Cell phones can be dangerous to your health. For a while, after their introduction into the world of business, doctors feared they might cause tumours inside the brain. It was a valid concern, considering the way everyone was walking around with a cell phone attached to their ear, tighter than lint to a wool dress. With all those little electrical currents passing through the ear canal into the brain, bombarding the same spot over and over, eighteen hours a day, it's a wonder cell phone users didn't develop a chain gang of tumours along their entire auditory system.

Then there are the automobile accidents caused by people talking on cell phones. It's enough to make you consider taking the bus.

There was one case of a woman talking on her car phone when she saw on the sidewalk a man who resembled her husband making out with a woman who was the spitting image of her best friend. The next minute her car veered to left of centre, careened off the bumper of a Smart Car and smashed into a lamp post that was supporting a hanging basket of flowers, which landed in her lap.

Fortunately, in the next few seconds, her husband miraculously showed up and was able to extricate her from the car without saying anything derogatory such as "Jeez, when are you going to learn how to drive?" And, can you believe her good luck? The next minute her best friend miraculously arrived on the scene, cooing and clucking little words of encouragement as she helped her from the wreckage. As the three of them surveyed the damage, they agreed it could have been a lot worse if the driver of the Smart Car had also been talking on a cell phone. In fact, when the police interviewed the driver of the Smart Car, he said he had never owned a cell phone and never intended to. For the woman involved in the accident, it was a defining moment, one that led to greater communion in her marriage. From that day forward, she never allowed her husband to go anywhere without her.

Another hazard of cell phone usage is the possibility of appearing rude. You know, you're sitting in a quiet restaurant with your dearly beloved, believing in your heart you are his one and only, and just as you are about to slurp up one of the oysters on a half shell, you notice a ringing in your ears. The next thing you know, the lips of your dearly beloved are moving – but not with little words of endearment. No. No. He is saying something like, "Yes, Joe. Put fifty bucks on 'Last Date' - across the board."

Cell phones have multiplied like laboratory rats. They can be found at the weekend cottage, inside the cabin of a 747 at 40,000 feet above sea level, on the seat of a farmer's pickup, hidden in the corner of a student's backpack. They have spread to every corner of the globe, to every country in the world.

Such as Finland. Here is a country with more cell phones per capita than any place in the world. In that country you can actually use your cell phone to dial the number of a vending machine. For instance, if you want a Finnish Delight Soda, you merely dial the appropriate number and your preferred brand of soda comes tumbling down the chute. Payment is a snap; the cost is simply added to your phone bill. What could be simpler and more convenient?

But this kind of thing can prove to be extremely dangerous. Suppose you are on your way home from work and you develop a hankering for a "Finnish Delight Chocolate Bar," but instead of dialling the number for your chosen treat, your finger accidentally slips and you dial "Finnish Delights Escort Service." You hang up immediately, of course, and re-dial the correct number. This should be the end of the story; but it isn't.

Three weeks later your cell phone bill arrives and your spouse is going through the listed calls to ensure you are only being charged for those that are legitimately yours. She notices a number that is unfamiliar and, since you are engrossed in a sports newscast covering the story of how Heikki Putemin has signed with the Vancouver Canucks in Canada for three million dollars, she decides to check out the number through information. I leave the rest of this situation to your imagination but, if you really think about it, can you imagine anything more dangerous?

Do you recall watching movies that were made before cell phones came along? Actors had to find a phone booth to make an important call and they were restricted in how far they could walk from the phone by the length of the cord. Today we've reached a point of virtual freedom from phone cords; yet we are more tied to our phones than ever.

Unfortunately, I can't discuss this subject any further. My cell phone is ringing.

THE CONNECTION BETWEEN LAWYERS AND THE SECOND LAW OF THERMODYNAMICS

One morning an absent-minded professor named Dr. Plank opened the door to his refrigerator and discovered that its contents resembled the floor of a west coast rain forest. That afternoon, when his wife sent him outside to repair the roof, he noticed all the shingles had more curls than Whoopi Goldberg. But it was later in the evening, when Dr. Plank pulled opened his sock drawer, that he began to form his hypothesis. Only two days before he had neatly arranged his socks in rows - black for gardening and puttering around the roof, white for business attire. But now he found the entire lot tangled and wrapped around each other in some kind of erotic sock-orgy. It was then Professor Plank formulated the second law of thermodynamics: things left to themselves will degenerate into disorder.

None of us need an absent-minded professor to tell us about disorder. We're all familiar with the way bathrooms revert to that state after being used by men, and the table in the hallway by the door that mysteriously accumulates debris without anyone ever having touched it. What about the drawer of your desk? You might spend an entire day organizing the contents and the minute you close it the brass tie tacks jump into an intimate relationship with the stickpins. I won't bother to elaborate on the clothes dryer, devouring socks and underwear as if it had some kind of dryer tapeworm. And then there are those hangers in the closet. You know how they clandestinely band together there in the darkness behind closed doors, so that the next time you try to pull out a single hanger you have to deal with the entire Hanger Union.

To call this phenomenon a law, however, is a misnomer. Laws are meant to **keep** order, not explain **dis**order. The truth is, disorder had its actual beginnings in law offices. I saw it first hand while I was working as a legal secretary. The problem is, lawyers are so busy interpreting the law and representing their clients that they don't have the time to attend to all those little everyday details, such as organizing their desks and files. That is why they hire secretaries and marry spouses.

One afternoon when my employer was in court interpreting and representing, I decided to tackle the mound of file folders that spread across his desk like decomposing straw bales. The lawyer always complained when I did this, claiming he could never find anything afterwards, but my need to organize had slipped into overdrive that day. It wasn't long before I discovered that his file folders had all formed illicit relationships with each other. I found the file of Lennie Lockton, felon and petty thief, hidden between the sheets of Ima Dunn's divorce papers. Under the dictaphone machine, where the lawyer kept a pile marked "pending," was an estate file labelled "I.M.Hardy." Mr Hardy had been dead for seven months and his heirs were getting anxious for distribution of the three million dollars he had left. Somehow his file had crawled under a copy of "Errors To Avoid When Making A Will." At the bottom of the pile on the desk I found a file marked, "Manley Shanks Mortgage." Manly Shanks was a big operator in the world of agriculture, so big, in fact, that he was always needing to borrow money to continue his farming operation. For some reason, his half-million-dollar mortgage file was tangled up with Busty Biggs' lap-dancing case. It took me a good two hours to unravel the lawyer's case files and stack them in neat piles in order of urgency but, even while I was doing so, I had this nagging feeling that they would all mix and mingle again the minute I turned my back.

Since I was well entrenched in the organizing mode, I decided to re-arrange his desk drawer. I picked up a paper clip that had strayed into the eraser section, but when I tried to return it to its former home, I discovered it was hanging out with a whole package of paper clips. Peer pressure is strong. As I pulled on a particular paper clip, its friends followed in loyal pursuit, forming an intricate chain that Cleopatra would have been proud to wear.

This started me thinking about chains and how we're all connected, which lead to thoughts about my family and the fact that we hadn't seen each other for some time. I decided, then and there, to organize a family reunion. We could all meet in Toronto. It is nice and central and most of my family know where it is. On Busty Biggs' cover I scratched the names of motels and hotels to contact, then I placed a sticky note on Lennie Lockton to remind me to call caterers in the Toronto area for full-course dinner quotes. I shoved Mr. Hardy's estate file back under the dictaphone to make room for my preliminary invitation list. The whole process of outlining my family get-together took up the rest of the afternoon and by the time I left the lawyer's office his desk looked as if it were once again covered with decomposing straw bales. At least he would be able to find everything.

SHE'S OSCILLATIN'

Back when a real, live Elvis was making his debut on the *Ed Sullivan Show*, if you looked in the back of your television set you could see an array of illuminated tubes that resembled the skyline of Toronto or Montreal. In those days, Toronto and Montreal were the only Canadian cities that *had* skylines. They were also the only Canadian cities that had NHL hockey teams.

Our local t.v. repair man, whom I'll call "Axel," had a single expression he used to describe the various afflictions which befell any television set in our community: "SHE'S OSCILLATIN'." It sounded impressive enough and I doubt anyone ever bothered to look up the word to see what it meant. It was easier and more expedient just to pay Axel's bill and get back to the *Ed Sullivan Show*.

In subsequent years I checked *Webster's New Collegiate Dictionary* for "oscillate" and, yes, I believe it had some relevance to Axel's diagnosis. It means "to move or travel back and forth between two points." I suppose those tubes could easily have heated up and started moving back and forth, thereby working themselves into a full-fledged "oscillation."

I found Axel's buzzword, however, had a second definition: "To vary between opposing beliefs, feelings or theories." As I contemplated these two meanings, I realized a lot of people I know could be classed as "oscillators."

My husband oscillates every time he goes fishing, running back and forth across the back of his boat between two salmon rods. This exemplifies definition number one. However, he is a double oscillator, constantly suffering the mental dilemma of choosing between two

31

opposing theories: "Fish or cut bait? Anchovies or hoochies? The Trap Shack or Beechey Head?"

My father was an oscillator too. Every time he planned a hunting trip it was: "Porcupine Ridge or Long Meadow? Cold sandwiches or hot *Chuckwagon Dinner?*" It appears most of the men in my family had an oscillation problem. When my cousin was in his prime he oscillated for a while between Joan and Cindy. He finally married Cindy. And then there's my youngest son, oscillating between hockey or football, baseball or golf. I have to admit I do a little oscillating myself at times. When I am sipping on a glass of cabernet I am dead certain it is *food* which causes weight gain, and each time I ingest a bowl of buttered popcorn or a plate of Nanaimo Bars, I know in my heart it is the *wine* I must leave alone.

Politicians are born oscillators. Remember when we didn't have the GST and then they gave us the GST and then they promised to remove the GST and then they reneged on their promise? Perhaps it all has something to do with the collective psyche of the Canadian public, seeing as how we have oscillated for nearly one hundred and forty years between the Liberals and Conservatives. And, speaking of Liberals and Conservatives, can you recall the last time a Member of Parliament oscillated between parties? I tell you, oscillation may be a truly Canadian phenomenon.

After I checked out "oscillate" I decided to research some other words that Axel might have used to diversify his t.v. jargon and maintain his position in the community as a specialist. I found:
"**vacillate**"- "to hesitate," which, I guess, is what he could have said when the t.v. didn't come on at all.
"**titillate**" - "to tickle, excite pleasurably." I don't know if this word was even in existence back in the days of tube-t.v. For some reason I thought it originated with Dolly Parton. Today I suppose it could be applied to any show on television, with *Survivor* providing the greatest titillation of all. The only thing I'm sure of is that none of us were very "tickled" when the t.v. oscillated in the middle of the *Ed Sullivan Show*.

"**palpitate**" - "beat rapidly and strongly". This has nothing to do with the operation of a television but if you are male, it probably happens to your heart muscle while viewing the female candidates on *Survivor*. It may also happen while watching Dolly. For me it occurs when I see Harrison Ford.

"**ululate**" - "to rise and fall in volume, pitch or cadence." This is a bit like "oscillate" except that it suggests a vertical rather than a horizontal movement. My father sometimes ululated, when he tried to call a moose in the middle of Long Meadow. As far as I know, there is no one on *Survivor* who ululates but Dolly certainly qualifies. Remember, though, it's only Dolly's voice that ululates.

"**speculate**" - "to meditate on or ponder," "to review something idly or casually." No doubt both *Survivor* and Dolly have often been the subject of male pondering, though neither has been reviewed idly or casually. Sometimes Axel "pondered and meditated" over our television for hours. It only seems appropriate that my parents also "reviewed idly and casually" his final bill.

IF THE RIGHT HAND OFFENDS, TRY THE LEFT

When I raise the subject of automatic writing, some of my friends look at me as though my brain had downloaded into my shoes. But I have been doing it most of my life. It started back in junior high, when I was a teenager. For no apparent reason, all my textbooks and scribblers began to sprout the letters "E.M. and P.J." Sometimes these letters were inscribed inside a heart. Then in grade eleven the writing changed. Suddenly, I found myself scribbling, "E.M. and W.W." inside the heart. And then, in my first year of college, the words, "I love J.R." started cropping up - on the inside cover of *Webster's Dictionary*, the back pages of my English text, throughout my psychology notebook. This persisted until August, 1961. That's when I married J.R.

I soon discovered that the family I had married into were automatic writers too. One day when I was cleaning out my husband's closet, I found one of his old high school text books and, there along the edge of the pages, written in large black letters was, "Live fast, love hard, die young." It was obvious his psychic talent had been inherited. Every time his father paid us a visit I would find little jottings - in the margins of newspapers, on the corners of the phone book, the paper napkin. Things like, "$20,000.00 @ 10% over 4 years..." or "$50,000.00 @ 15% compounded monthly =..."

The tendency spread to my children. One summer our family camped out in a small travel trailer while we built a house in the country. Toilet facilities were provided by a little red outhouse constructed by my father-in-law. Before a week was out, its inner walls suddenly erupted with quotations. From our 12-year-old son, who happens to have the same initials as his father: "Here lies what's left of J.R." Our 11-year-old daughter: "If you don't eat your supper you don't get anything else." And, not surprisingly, from my father-in-law: "Two-holer - $129.95."

As my children entered young adulthood, their skill for automatic writing became more pronounced. In my son's school textbooks I found little poems which should have forewarned me he was destined to become a sailor. My daughter's aversion to historical data was obvious by this entry made in her history notebook: "I'm going to DIE in this class!" The words were surrounded by sketches of wedding gowns.

By the time my children left home to follow their own lives, I began to wonder if I had lost my own ability to interpret the spirit world. I bought a copy of *How To Do Automatic Writing* and set about following the step by step instructions. "First you must clear out any negative energy. This can be done by lighting candles, burning incense or saying a mantra." I lit two candles on my office desk, sat down and assumed a relaxed posture, pen held lightly in my hand. Closing my eyes, I could feel the energy flow through me, down my arm and into my hand. I wrote something. I opened my eyes to see what great knowledge I had channelled. "For a good time call..."

Obviously I hadn't dispersed all the negative energy. I needed more artillery. Some incense should do the trick. I lit a cone of sandalwood and tried once more. This time I found myself drawing little cartoon characters in medieval costume with the caption, "The king is a fink!"

A mantra. I needed a mantra. I closed my eyes once again and began to sway back and forth, singing softly, over and over:
"I's the b'ye that built the boat,
And I's the b'ye that sails 'er."
Suddenly my whole body was encased in a powerful sensation. The next moment I became a psychic vehicle, ready to convey to the world a message of such profundity, such deep and lasting wisdom, that I would be heralded in future centuries as a prophet. Pen touched paper. Black rings appeared as my hand began making little circular

motions. My breath was coming in short, raspy puffs, my skin was on fire, my toes tingling. And then, in a scroll of erratic black letters, galloping across a white page, it came: "Those who know do not tell and those who tell do not know."

I crumpled up the paper and threw it on the floor. Who needs to be a prophet anyhow? I decided to stick to more worldly subjects. Picking up the pen once more, I took a new sheet of paper and wrote, "I love J.R."

IS IT REALLY EWE?

What remarkable things have happened in the scientific world. First we had Dolly, the cloned sheep, then it was glow-in-the-dark mice, the Pathfinder landing on Mars, and levitated frogs.

The mechanics required to levitate a frog are beyond my limited knowledge, but I think I have the basics of cloning figured out.

It all started in 1996 when Dr. Ian Wilmut was wandering aimlessly through the Scottish highlands and he happened to come across a lone sheep. "Only one sheep," he thought. "One *never* sees a single sheep." Dr. Wilmut knew something was definitely wrong in the cosmos. He set out to create more sheep. This should not be considered peculiar for a scientist who is a native of the country responsible for haggis and curling.

With a pail of first-grade barley he enticed a Finn Dorset ewe into his laboratory, the Roslin Institute, near Edinburgh, wherein he removed some cells from her udder. Where were the animal rights people when this was taking place, I hear you wondering? Why were they not protecting Ms. Dorset's honour? Well, the truth is that Dr. Wilmut and his team of embryologists were working so quietly, so surreptitiously on this project that the rest of world knew nothing about it.

The cells from Ms. Dorset's udder were placed in a petri dish and deprived of nutrients, whereby they stopped dividing and fell into a state of slumber. It has been proven by previous scientific experimentation that the reproductive act is the furthest thing from the human mind when that human is hungry. But, pour that human a glass of cabernet, serve up a fine meal, perhaps throw in a crackling fire and...well, who knows what may happen?

Meanwhile, back at the lab, Dr. Wilmut was up to his old tricks, only this time he was stealing eggs from a Blackface ewe. He schlucked (yes "schlucked") the nucleus, together with all of its DNA, out of a purloined egg, leaving only the empty shell. Next, he took Ms. Dorset's sleepy cell, which was making gross snoring noises in the petrie dish, and placed it beside the empty one from Ms. Blackface. Finally, he zapped them with his stock prod - the one he carries with him in the highlands in case he encounters an angry bull.

The sleepy cell woke with a start and jumped into the first available relationship she found, straight into Ms. Blackface's empty egg cell "and the two became one." Cell division took off like a hot mining stock and in a few days produced a lovely little Blackface-Dorset embryo, which Dr. Wilmut then implanted into the udder of a second Blackface ewe. (What happened to the first Ms. Blackface? Will she forever be a "painted lady"?)

Finally, after a respectable gestation period during which Dr. Wilmut resumed his highland wandering, a tiny, perfectly-formed baby lamb was born, genetically identical to Ms. Dorset. "It's a girl!" was the wire Dr. Wilmut received from the Institute as he was warming up in a stone castle with a glass of Scotch. They named her Dolly.

That's the way the story was written in *Macleans,* believe it or not. Sometimes I wonder if it is really a fairy tale. I mean, if Ian was going to clone a species, why didn't he choose something more interesting than a sheep, something with enough diversities to make it truly unique and easily recognizable to all, like haggis or curling. On second thought, though, I guess one haggis is as bad as any other and eventually curlers all begin to look, act, and talk alike. At present I am still not convinced that Dolly is anything other than an ordinary sheep produced in that traditional way i.e. after an evening of good food, fine wine and a crackling fire.

Mary had a little lamb
It never knew its mother
That's because it was a clone
And looked like any udder.
Jeff Robbins

I DON'T WANNA BE A WILDEBEEST

There's a lot of interest these days in alternative medicine and it also appears that various forms of religion are gaining popularity. One I especially find intriguing is reincarnation, the idea that we come back to live again. A chance to do it over. In fact, it is my understanding that reincarnationists keep coming back until they get it right, and when that happens, they finally go on to the state of Nirvana. Think about some of the people you have known. Don't you think they will be required to come back, perhaps more than once? The bigger question might be, "Who will live with them next time?"

Suppose, however, that we don't come back as humans but as animals. Will we have a choice? If so, what would it be? The snake, no doubt, will be at the bottom of the list with the lion placing somewhere near the top. Pampered cats? There's probably a waiting list. Goldfish? Not a nibble. Who wants to spend their life in a fish bowl? Just ask any celebrity.

I've always believed that it's easier to discover what you want if you first know what you don't want, and there is one species I *definitely* wouldn't want to become; a wildebeest. For one thing, a wildebeest is also known as a "brindled gnu." Who wants to go through life as a brindled gnu?

Attractiveness definitely does not play a big part in your life if you are a wildebeest. Not when you have a mane, a beard, heavy curved horns, you stand 1.4 metres tall and weigh about 270 kg. (600 lb.) It's hard to understand how wildebeests reach such enormous weights because they are always running, running, running. You've seen them on all those nature shows, madly galloping across the African plains, pursued by some fleet-of-foot four-legged creature, usually some species of cat. Everything chases wildebeests; lions, tigers, hyenas, cheetahs, panthers, leopards. And every wildebeest gets caught. Perhaps it's because of the 600 lbs. they carry around on that 1.4 metre frame.

Humans spend a great deal of time and mental energy searching for their purpose in life. For the wildebeest there is no such emotional quandary. Its purpose is, purely and simply, to be eaten. It's as if this animal wears some obscure bumper sticker that says, "Have you eaten your wildebeest today?" And it seems the wildebeest knows this because it never puts up a struggle. Once a tiger or a cheetah sinks its fangs into the wildebeest, the animal falls over, ker-chonk, without a snarl or a sneer. You'd think it would at least try to dig out one or two tiger-eyes or knock a few spots off that annoying leopard before cashing in.

The wildebeest doesn't warrant much space in the encyclopaedia either. In the *Academic American* version it comes between "Oscar Wilde" and "Laura Ingalls Wilder," which is an impressive place to be if you are an author. In the dictionary there is more space given to "wildcat" than there is to "wildebeest." But then, why waste a lot of paper on something that is going to get eaten anyhow.

I guess, with my Baptist upbringing, I should be careful about delving into this reincarnation stuff. Besides, I can't imagine how I would make it to church if I weighed six hundred pounds.

KEEP THE LIGHTS ON WITH BEANS

The future of the world lies with the bean-eaters. With oil reserves dwindling, we human beings must look to alternate sources of energy to heat and cool our homes and propel our sports utility vehicles back and forth across freeways during a lane change. A kilowatt of electricity is more expensive than a package of McCain's frozen fiddleheads and nuclear power has the potential to blow us into orbit alongside Timothy Leary. That leaves natural gas, a substance that is colourless, odourless, and tasteless, and seems to be found mostly in Alberta. Unfortunately, the supply of natural gas, like any of nature's resources, is finite. There is, however, one place where an infinite supply exists - on the east coast of Canada, following the consumption of copious quantities of beans every Saturday night. After growing up in New Brunswick I can speak as one who has "bean there, done that." But let's be serious. This reliable, renewable source of energy could well be the answer to Canada's energy requirements through the next twenty-seven referendums.

The creation of natural gas is so important to the operation of the universe that, just fourteen days after fertilization of a human egg (or two weeks after the big night, whichever comes first), the intestinal tract is formed in the embryo - even before the development of a heart, lungs, kidneys or gall bladder. It starts in something called the endoderm. Little cells in the endoderm hold a quick referendum and decide to separate. No, no, that's not it. That comes later. These endoderm cells actually decide to form something called a cavity. For years, anatomists simply referred to this as a "cavity," until one day a student of archaeology suggested a more technical term: Primitive Gut.

Of course, the word "primitive" indicates that something more advanced will follow. This is the place to talk about separation. After three weeks, the primitive gut differentiates into three parts, The Maritime Provinces, Quebec and Ontario, and The West. No, no. Wrong again. I meant to write: The foregut, midgut, and hindgut. Whoever said anatomy was difficult?

The foregut is composed of the upper digestive tract, including the stomach, so that if you suddenly feel the need for a tablespoon of Mylanta it is entirely correct to say, "I have a disturbance in my foregut." The hindgut gets short shrift in the anatomy books, one line explaining that it is "the remainder of the large intestine." This does not mean it is unimportant; merely unmentionable. Between the foregut and the hindgut lies the midgut, the section responsible for all those Gas X television commercials. You may remember from your Grade Six health class that the midgut contains five miles of small intestine with more convolutions than a new perm.

This is how it all works. Suppose at 6:00 p.m. you scarf down two quarter pounders with cheese, a large plate of poutine, a soft drink and half a dozen Tim Horton's doughnuts. When the burgers and their entourage reach your stomach, they are attacked by an army of digestive enzymes bent on ethnic cleansing. These little enzymes proceed to beat into mush every smidgen of meat, wheat, or sweet, so that, after a period of four hours, if one were to examine the stomach, they would be unable to tell if the contents had originated at McDonald's, Burger King, Wendy's or Tim Horton's.

Are you still with me? It's only 10:00 p.m.

This transformation of burgers, poutine and doughnuts into something that resembles liquid junk results in the creation of natural gas in the intestine, or midgut (remember your anatomy?)

Anatomists began looking for a highly technical term for this process of human gas production. After the third ballot, they opted for "flatus." Unfortunately, the gas produced by flatus is unlike its geological counterpart in Alberta in a number of respects: it is far from odourless and is definitely not tasteless, particularly when confined to a small space such as an elevator or a church pew.

But I must not allow personal opinion to taint a highly scientific hypothesis. Let us view this through the eyes of a mathematician. If X creates a half litre of gas per meal, providing X eats three times a day, how many litres will be created by thirty million Canadians in one day, provided they eat three meals a day? The answer is: 45,000,000 litres. Our calculation is basic in the extreme and does not take into consideration stolen hourly snacks, or the nation-wide guzzlement of beer and pickled eggs by all those Joe Canadians.

This mathematical conclusion is based on the normal, everyday eating habits of Canadians. In New Brunswick, however, the situation differs. All because of the Saturday Night Bean Tradition. When people from New Brunswick say they were "raised on beans," they are speaking an absolute truth. In fact, beans are what make them a "distinct society." How well I remember the ritual surrounding our tradition: the crucial overnight soak; the diligent blending, on Saturday morning, of important ingredients such as onions, molasses, and salt pork; the tempting all-day smell of baking beans; and, finally, the intrinsic joy of munching down several plates of beans along with slices of homemade brown bread, fresh from the oven. To have grown up on beans, can there be a greater heritage?

There I go again, waxing nostalgic. I must remember this is a serious treatise, one on which the future of mankind may well depend. What I am attempting to bring to your attention is that in New Brunswick there is a cheap, easily obtainable surplus of natural gas. (This may also apply to the other three Maritime provinces; however, since any visits I made to them occurred on weekdays, I am not qualified to comment on their Saturday night eating habits. I will stick with what I know - New Brunswick.)

Now we must go back to mathematics. If a New Brunswicker named X produces five times the normal amount of natural gas on a Saturday night and there are Y people in New Brunswick on any given Saturday night, how much natural gas is produced in a year? The answer is staggering. Just ask any Moosehead drinker.

With this supply of ready, reliable, and renewable energy, New Brunswick may well be the centre of the next economic BOOM. In no time they'll have their own bumper stickers:

"BEANS are forever."

"Who needs Hibernia, we've got BEANS!"

"I'm proud to be a BEANEATER!"

"The rest of Canada doesn't know BEANS!"

"Life in New Brunswick is a gas."

"Light up your life with BEANS."

"Move over, Irving. BEANS are here."

"Happiness is owning a BEAN crock."

"Make flatus, not war."

"Let the westerners freeze in the dark."

"The last one out of British Columbia, please turn out the lights."

And one day down the road, when our nation is no longer at the mercy of oil cartels, when we are able to cosy up to our Flatus Fireplaces and stir up some McCain's SuperFries in an oven heated by N.B. RealGas, when it becomes possible to drive our sports utility vehicles from Newfoundland to Carrot River for the cost of three-day-old bread, some prominent spokesperson will stand up in the New Brunswick legislature- perhaps even the Premier himself (or herself) - and make a statement that will go down in history as one of the great quotes of all time: "Never, in the history of mankind, has so much been produced by so few for so many."

THE CONSTANT THAT BINDS
CANADIANS TOGETHER

The *Canadian Encyclopaedia* states, "television is the one thing most Canadians have in common." There is one other thing that Canadians have in common and it also begins with the letter T - Taxes. This is how the encyclopaedia describes taxation: "Compulsory payments by individuals and corporations to government, levied to finance government services, to redistribute income and to influence the behaviour of consumers and investors." Indeed, it appears that since the Canadian parliament was given unlimited powers of taxation in 1867, the taxation train has turned into one big gravy train for our government.

In order to carry out the collection of all these taxes, Parliament needs tax collectors. But not just anyone can perform such a daunting task. Tax collector wannabes must undergo an intensive training process - Taxation 101% - where they will learn all about horizontal equity, vertical equity, revenue elasticity, redistribution, influencing behaviour and indexing.

redistribution: This course is better known as Taxation 50/50. The student learns how to collect 50% of an individual's income after he or she has already paid out 49% of income in property tax, sales tax, and Goods and Services Tax, i.e. GST. This collected 50% is redistributed among the politicians. One of the exercises the tax collector student completes for this course is:

Pairs of students are given 100 poker chips – "A" represents the taxpayer and "B" is the government. The question is worded thus: If A has 100 poker chips and he is required to give half of his poker chips to B for redistribution, how will A be sure he can actually receive at least one poker chip back? Answer: He can't.

Question 2: If A has 100 poker chips and is required to give the greatest percentage of them to B whose job is to redistribute them to C, how many poker chips will C receive?
Answer: It all depends on how many poker chips A is able to keep for himself without B knowing about it.

The tax collector student has a profound challenge to separate A from 50 of his poker chips. A is begrudgingly allowed a personal exemption, which is enough to buy a month's supply of Tylenol. If A is married he or she is allowed a larger exemption, after paying for a marriage licence, of course. If A is lucky enough to have offspring, the amount of the exemption increases with the birth of each child so that by the birth of the fourth child, A can claim an amount equal to a month's supply of Tylenol and a case of disposable diapers. Owning a dog does not allow you to qualify for an exemption, only the necessity of paying a dog licence fee.

Someone of prominence once said, "The more you give, the more you have." That person did not live in Canada.

With the concept of redistribution under wraps, students move on to the psychological part of the Taxation 101% course.

Influencing Behaviour.

They are taught that the most effective way to reduce inflation is by reduction of private spending and such reduction can be effected simply by imposing more tax. Who said taxation was complicated? One of the exercises in this section of the taxation course involves a balloon and a vice. The balloon is labelled "public spending" and the student, after blowing up the balloon to its full extent, places it in a vice marked "TAX." By turning the screws on the vice and increasing pressure on the balloon, the student is finally able to break the balloon, reducing private spending to mere shreds of its former self. Inflation is merely a memory. The only thing left intact in its previous form is the tax. This proves that TAX is the only constant.

Next comes the most difficult part of Taxation 101%, a study of revenue elasticity. This is the percentage change in tax revenue resulting in a change of national income. What students find is that, regardless of any changes that may take place in national income, even in the likely event of a reduction in take-home pay, taxation remains the same, leading to a confirmation of our earlier deduction that the only constant is TAX.

The last part of the taxation course involves something we all learned in public school when our teachers insisted on an outline for everything we passed in. We were even encouraged to create an outline for our lunch. In taxation terms this is called indexing. The tax student ends up with an index that looks something like this:

Index for Taxation 101%
> definition of taxation
> origin of taxation
> purpose of taxation
> redistribution of tax revenue
> influencing behaviour with taxation
> revenue elasticity
> conclusion: Universal constant - TAX

At the successful conclusion of the course, the student will receive a diploma with his or her name in Latin and the awesome title of TAX COLLECTOR written in Old English script. They are now qualified for a job in the Department of Finance or, more likely, in the offices of Revenue Canada.

A student may want to advance their education, however, and pursue their studies further into the EXTRA TAX field: Surtax, Luxury Tax, and Excise Tax, to name only a few. Or they may wish to specialize exclusively in the Underground Economy, a phenomenon that has resulted from the GST. This will require some extensive training in the art of espionage and perhaps a black belt in snooping.

Not everyone is cut out to be a tax collector and certainly not every person is able to grasp all the concepts involved. You must possess TM, i.e. a Taxation Mentality. If you find the tax arena is not to your liking, you may be more suited to a career in Fee Setting. The possibilities for advancement in this area are endless: Eco fees on paint cans, spray bombs, batteries, rat poison and concrete, in addition to licensing fees for every possible acquisition or pursuit the ordinary Canadian may choose or indulge in. Add to this the lucrative area of fuel surcharges imposed by airlines, ferry systems, and Canada Post and you have a guaranteed career, all the way to pension.

HOW TO OUTPACK AN ALPACA

There has been a lot of hype about llamas and alpacas and their ability to be used as pack animals. According to alpaca aficionados, these animals eat less than a horse, are more easily managed, and can carry up to 60 pounds of gear. They are also gentle, predictable, and affectionate - they love to kiss your face - and they don't whinny. Of course, everything has a downside and I would be remiss as a writer if I didn't present both sides of the cookie. Llamas have one bad habit. They spit.

But there is another species that may well send these two pack animals packing. I'm talking about the 130-pound woman with a purse. Why is it that women insist on hauling around a leather pouch that exceeds the carry-on limit on an aircraft when men seem to get by just fine with a wallet and a comb? I've tried to lighten up, to be more like the men, but each time I left my purse at home I felt so...naked.

I don't think the rest of the world realizes the horse power that is expended every day by women carrying purses. For my husband, the revelation came when I asked him to hold my purse while I unlocked the door. He lurched forward, barely catching himself on the doorjamb. "WHAT do you have in here?" he asked. "No wonder you have shoulder problems."

One day, after I had complained, yet again, of a lame shoulder, he offered some "purse therapy."

"You need to lighten up," he said. "Let me help you do a little purse downsizing."

We dumped the contents out on the table, then made two lists: "Need," and, "Don't Need."

Under "Need" we put:

> money - in case I need to shop
> Canadian Tire money - in case I need to shop at Canadian Tire
> loonies - in case I need to park
> glasses - in case I need to see
> *his* glasses - in case *he* needs to see
> lipstick - in case I need to be seen
> umbrella - in case it rains
> sun glasses - in case it stops raining
> crackers - in case I need to eat
> toothbrush and toothpaste - in case I need to eat out
> antacids - in case I eat too much
> breath mints - in case I need to talk
> gum - in case the mints don't work
> acetaminophen - in case I get a headache from eating or talking

We decided that these items could stay. However, there were other things - Band-Aids, guitar picks, spare panty hose, camera film, a Nana Miskouri tape, and a broken watch band - that he put in the "Don't Need" pile. "Now, about this little bottle of cayenne pepper," he said. "Why is that in there?"

"Because," I answered, "I read in my *10 Essential Herbs* book that if you come across an accident and the victim is unconscious, you can often revive them with a few grains of cayenne placed under the tongue."

"You could also be sued," he said, placing the cayenne in the "Don't Need" pile.

He looked at the two piles with smug satisfaction. "Now your purse will be a lot lighter," he said, as he started putting all the "Need" articles - *his* glasses in particular - back in. After he had left, I picked up everything else on the table and dumped it into the purse, comforted by the fact that, if times ever get tough, I can hire out to a hiking company. My resume will read: "gentle, manageable, affectionate, carrying capacity - 75 pounds, equipped with first aid supplies such as Band-Aids and cayenne pepper. Does not spit."

THE PERPLEXING PECULARITIES
OF MALE BEHAVIOUR

What is it about the male species? They can't walk down a hallway without causing all the pictures on the wall to hang at half-mast. Then there's the bathroom at the end of that hallway. When they leave it, it resembles a war zone; the toilet seat has been held up, there's enough shaving cream on the mirror to handle an emergency landing of a jumbo jet, and all the towels look as if they have been assaulted.

Once he's showered and shaved (no easy thing to convince him to do) a man undertakes to dress himself. If you have a four poster bed you know that a man can almost always turn it into his own personal valet, particularly for organizing those little articles that might otherwise get lost in the shuffle, such as socks and jock shorts. In fact, there have been cases of men with a military background actually saluting a pair of red boxer shorts that were draped over the foot post of their bed.

Then there's the dresser in the corner. Let a man come within two feet of it and suddenly it looks as though he has been steppe farming. All the drawers resemble terraces filled to overflowing with trailing lobelia. But these are only the remains of the socks and shorts that don't make it to the four poster bed.

Something else occurs in the bedroom when a man removes his trousers. Wait a minute! It's far from erotic or sensual, unless you become aroused watching someone handle loose change, crumpled bits of paper, a wallet, a comb, and a tangled assortment of keys - to the house, workshop, office, and a '57 Chevy. These are the objects he pulls out of his pockets and places on top of the dresser, just before the lights go out. Oh, he could put them in the little dresser-top valet you gave him for Christmas - the one with the little drawer in it. That is, if it wasn't filled with old credit cards, more loose change, two watches that don't work, a cuff link with no mate, and the hood ornament from that '57 Chevy.

All of this is normal behaviour for a man. In fact, if the man in your life ever deviates from this pattern, take him to the emergency department of the hospital immediately. Of course, you will have to take a number, but this may give just enough time for him to come to his senses. After he has rifled through the neatly layered magazines on the emergency room table he should be back to normal.

Anyhow, we of the female species must learn to live around this if we are to survive. I suggest a few inventions to make our situation a little less stressful.

For the hallway: Install Velcro on the back of each picture and glue its counter-piece to the wall.

For the bathroom: How about a giant windshield wiper blade installed at the top of the bathroom mirror. A little flick of a switch and, voila, the mirror is sparkling clean for the next user. For the toilet seat, install a button above the toilet tank marked with the letter "M" for "male" and a digital dial underneath. The male punches in the time he will need for his ablutions. Then at the end of that time, the toilet seat, by means of a spring, snaps back down into its former position. This little installation alone will save at least 60% of relationships. The spring can be used on the towels as well. The hand towel is permanently attached to the wall and as soon as a man finishes with one, it snaps back automatically into its little niche in the wall, neatly folded, ready for the next user. Bath towels are also attached to the wall and after their third use a little light flashes above them, indicating it is time for the laundry.

And now for the bed/valet dilemma. Perhaps the posts can be wired with some kind of an automated audio system. When a man hangs something on the bedpost and covers up one of its sensitivity points, an alarm will sound. The same alarm idea might be applied to dresser drawers if the drawers remain open after a pre-ordained period of time. To make it even more effective and add a little levity, the alarm might include a voice, perhaps that of Yosemite Sam shouting, "Say your prayers, Varmit."

The matter of males not putting things back on closet shelves can be solved by a contraption that acts like a reverse bungy cord, attached to each article on the shelves. This will allow a man to pull down a box and examine its contents, then, when he is finished pawing through it, the box will automatically retract back to its original position. Another 30% of relationships saved.

These are only a few of the relationship-saving devices that might be implemented in a household containing a male and a female. In fact, some of them would make great wedding gifts. Spending a few extra dollars on one of these inventions now may insure that you get invited to the couple's 25th. By then he will be so well trained it won't matter that the warranty has long since expired.

THE CONSPIRACY THEORY - THE TRUTH AT LAST!

Q. Why did Moses spend forty years wandering in the wilderness?
A. He wouldn't ask for directions.

I knew exactly how Mrs. Moses felt on the day we drove into Medicine Hat, Alberta, in search of our friends, Dave and Shirley. It was 1:30 in the afternoon when we reached the outskirts of the city. My husband was whistling, our two children were sleeping peacefully in the back seat of the car, and I was looking forward to some long overdue girl talk with Shirley.

At 3:30, not only were we still looking for Dave and Shirley, we were getting low on gas. When we drove past the same service station for the fourth time, I began to form an opinion. We were lost. But the "L" word is not one that is spoken in a car containing a man whose face is the colour of an American Beauty Rose.

As I cast a longing eye to the pay phone zipping past, I began to wonder. Is it the same for males in all species? What about geese? Think about it. There's the gander, winging his way along the foothills of the Rockies, when his lifelong mate sidles up to him and whispers, "Isn't that the same Calgary Tower we flew over two hours ago?" Instantly he gets into a big flap and honks at her, "Shut up and fly!"

No, this would never happen in the animal world. Animals are born with a locator-gene, a kind of mini-computer in their brain and they always know exactly where they are going. But in baby boy-humans, this locator-gene self destructs at the moment of birth, along with all association with the word "lost." If you don't believe me, just ask yourself when was the last time you heard a male person use the "L" word? You'll find it simply doesn't exist in their vocabulary. Little boys may wander and meander; ramble and roam, straggle and stray. They may often be late for supper; but they are never, ever, **LOST.**

I remember all those times my father came home late from hunting. "Were you lost?" my mother would ask, whereby he always offered the same explanation: "No. I just got turned around."

I was thinking about all of this when my husband yanked on the steering wheel and roared up to a gas pump. He jumped out of the car, grabbed the nozzle and jammed it into the tank.

Are we lost?" asked our six-year-old daughter.

"Naw," said her brother, "we're just turned around."

When my husband got back into the car I decided to "go for it." I broached my suggestion as carefully as one sets a mousetrap. "Do you suppose we should ask Somme for directions?" I said, holding forth the crumpled piece of paper with the words "Dave & Shirley" and an address scribbled beneath. His mouth looked as if it had been drawn with a felt pen and a ruler. Our children were trying to act invisible.

Finally, I decided to tell him something that has been secret for too long - about the gene that baby girls develop which is responsible for the conspiracy. This gene lies dormant for about seventeen years or until a female enters into a relationship with a male, whichever happens first. Then the conspiratorial behaviour begins to emerge. Women secretly take drafting courses at nights where they learn to alter maps, and at those times when men are absorbed in the world of t.v., females change all the street signs. Oh, not so anyone would really notice. They only give them a quarter turn - but it is enough. It is a practice that has kept males wandering in circles since the days of Moses. It is nature's way of creating a balance between the sexes.

It's not that women never get lost. They just don't *stay* lost for long. Women will ask questions. I've done it. Last summer in Edmonton, Alberta, I took a wrong turn off the Whitemud Freeway and ended up in an unfamiliar part of the city. Undaunted, I drove into the first service station I saw. There were three men draped over the gas pump. Actually they looked as if they had been there since the last big snow. My sister rolled down the window and smiled.

"We're lost," she said. Two of the men ignored us. The third, the one closest to the car window, unwound himself from the pump and smiled back.

"Oh, you'll find your way," he said, wandering off.

I think the males in Edmonton may have heard about the drafting courses and the sign shifting.

THE LASTING EFFECTS
OF SNAKE DANGLING

My fear of snakes was imprinted at the age of five, in the way most little girl's fears are imprinted - by little boys. His name was Arvard. Arvard and his two sisters lived down the road in a little white clapboard house surrounded by bush. His sisters were my playmates and we all simply "put up" with Arvard, who was four years older.

I'll never forget the day I became an ophidiophobiac. We were playing Roy Rogers and Dale Evans in the hardwood trees and suddenly, out of the corner of my eye, I caught a movement - several movements to be exact. There was Arvard, a writhing, curling rope of garter green dangling from his hand, advancing toward me with a look on his square little face that might have sent Frankenstein's monster running for its mother. Fortunately, I had been blessed with a strong pair of legs and an equally strong set of lungs. Three eternities later, Arvard's mother appeared with an expression that could have sent Frankenstein's monster scrambling for its soother. She grabbed Arvard's ear with one hand and the snake in the other, threw the snake into the woods and propelled her wayward son all the way to the house using only a shoe (with her foot still in it.) But the damage had been done. I had a confirmed case of ophidiophobia.

It was also from Arvard that I acquired claustrophobia. One day after the snake incident we were all playing hide and seek. I jumped into the empty woodbox and closed the lid. The perfect hiding place. Then Arvard found me. Just as I attempted to climb out of the woodbox, he slammed the cover down and sat on it. For three eternities he sat there while I screamed through the slits in the sides and cried into the sawdust. It wasn't until I neared a state of hysteria that he decided to let me out, leaving me with a lifelong dread of woodboxes, airplanes and elevators.

I have thought long and hard about little boys who emotionally impact little girls' psyche for life by being little jerks and I propose the following retribution. Young Arvards who do nasty and insensitive things shall be dressed in a shirt and tie and pilloried for a day, forced to listen to a full seven hours of classical music and selections from Shelley and Keats. Every fifteen minutes, a little girl will wash his face with warm water and lots and lots of soap, followed by another little girl who will comb his hair and stick it into place. Every hour on the hour, he will be tickled by silk ribbons and sprayed with cologne by a member of the Red Hat Society. Hopefully, this will put an end to the snake and woodbox incidents.

Retributive justice, if only on paper, brings its own sense of balance. I feel better already. I can now tell you the "rest of the story" about my childhood nemesis.

Somehow, one hot summer afternoon, Arvard happened upon a nickel (perhaps one just fell into his hand off his parents' dresser). He bought a package of Old Dutch potato chips - the kind in the foil bag that rustled - and then called his sisters and I under the front steps. "These are potato chips," he said, ripping open the bag with his jacknife. At first we were sceptical. It could very well have contained rabbit or deer droppings. But after Arvard munched down a few, he passed one to each of us. I popped it in my mouth. Suddenly, every sensate cell in my olfactory system opened up like a peony on an anthill. Crisp and light and salty and potato-y and yet not any of these in particular, it was without a doubt the most profoundly delicious taste experience of my young life. I had been exposed to the world of potato chips and nothing would ever be the same again. All because of Arvard. I don't know why he shared them with us. Perhaps it was guilt over the way he had acquired the nickel. Or perhaps, somewhere inside that nasty little snake-dangling, woodbox-sitting monster, there actually was a heart. After all, students of biology know that even toads have hearts.

REAL COGITATION IS FOR MALES ONLY

By now we have all accepted the fact that men have four billion more brain cells than women. But one thing bothers me about this experiment: it was carried out on another continent - Denmark to be exact. So I am wondering, do their findings also apply to North Americans or are they restricted to Danes only? Is this where the term Great Dane originated?

It doesn't really bother me that men reputedly have more brain cells than women. Actually, the discovery confirms something we women have long suspected: that men are overqualified - to think.

You see examples of this overqualification every day. Of course a man with that many extra brain cells cannot possibly be expected to stoop over and pick up something as ordinary as a pair of socks or the jock shorts he draped over the bed railing last night. It would make him top heavy, to say the least, not to mention the fact that he might scramble some important cerebral connections. And how can a man ever remember to wipe the shaving foam off the bathroom mirror while he ponders questions of such magnitude as "Will the Oilers beat the Leafs on Saturday?"or "I wonder why in God's name the Canucks hired *him* as coach?"

It is this great encumbrance of extra brain cells that is responsible for men needing a cerebral break, i.e. a beer break - two every evening before dinner, half a dozen on a Friday night and one every fifteen minutes during a t.v. sports event on Saturdays. Without this opportunity to put all those surplus cells into a comatose state, a man could just about go crazy with thinking. In fact, it is possible he could be kept in a perpetual state of time-and-a-half cogitation, without the benefit of an organized union.

The excess brain power plays a particularly prominent role in the matter of travel destinations. You see, at least half of these four billion brain cells are imprinted with road maps. In fact, if you sliced into one you'd be apt to discover places like Wawa, Ontario, Quispamsis, New Brunswick, or Zabellos, British Columbia, but unfortunately, because of the overwhelming number of cells, the ability to actually *find* Wawa, Ontario, Quispamsis, New Brunswick, or Zabellos, British Columbia is somewhat impaired, making it nearly impossible for any male to ever find his way there, or to anyplace else for that matter. Of course, he could stop and ask someone for directions but, I ask you, with four billion extra brain cells, is that an insult to your intelligence or what?

This imbalance in the brain cell count between men and women can cause problems in relationships. Take the case of Dean and Louise. When they first met, all of Dean's brain cells - not only just the four billion extra but ALL - mutated, creating a person who was unrecognizable to his friends and family. He did and said things not in keeping with a responsible adult. Everyone chalked it up to something called "love."

But after a time, Dean settled down, content to channel his extra brain power into creating ingenious methods to beat the blackjack tables on those periodic trips to Vegas. As he arranged for a new line of credit, Louise kept plugging away at more trivial pursuits, such as planting and harvesting a vegetable garden, canning, pickling and preserving, sewing Barbie clothes for her daughter, driving the boys to hockey practice, painting the house inside and out, cooking and doing laundry for a family of five. After twenty years of observing this, Dean couldn't stand it any more. He took up with another woman. It's tough to satisfy someone who has a four-billion brain cell advantage.

Did I clarify that Dean is not a Dane? I should have done that right away. You probably know someone exactly like him. Right here in North America. Anyhow, the next time you meet a tourist from Denmark, ask him if he knows the way to Wawa, Ontario, Quispamsis, New Brunswick, or Zabellos, British Columbia.

ONLY MEN GET TYW SYNDROME

A friend of ours recently succumbed to TYW. This is not to be confused with TMJ (temperomandibular joint disorder), which is associated with jaw clenching, although with TYW jaw clenching may be a side effect. TYW afflicts males over 30 and can often cause its victims to be bedridden. The carriers of this malaise are not viruses or microbes; rather, it is transmitted by women - younger women. Hence the name TYW (The Younger Woman) Syndrome. Males who have passed the big 50 are extremely susceptible, which is what happened to our friend, Mick.

Thirty-five years ago Mick stood up with us at our wedding, along with his wife, Missey. Mick and Missey. They were the ideal couple. That is, until two years ago, when TYW struck. Mick left for Nova Scotia with his guitar and his velvet painting and Missey sold their house and bought an oceanfront condo.

Last summer we received a call from Mick. He was in town visiting and would like us to meet his new wife. They showed up just after lunch, in a Ferrari as red as Julia Roberts' lips in the movie, *Pretty Woman*. Mick looked as if he had stumbled into a fountain of Rogaine. He had hair - dark brown hair, and the waistline that had once won him a prize for having the longest belt had shrunk like last month's party balloon. Then he stepped aside to reveal Twyla. At first I thought he said "Delilah," but sometimes I don't hear as well as I should.

Twyla had more hair than a Chia Pet and it was the colour of Chardonnay wine. She looked so young I didn't know whether to shake her hand or take her on my knee. She flashed a smile, made a fan movement with her hand and said, "Hi." As I followed her into the living room I marvelled at her footwear. Twyla could have driven fence posts with the heels on her platform shoes.

We talked for a while, or, rather, we didn't talk for a while. It seemed that every time I wanted to ask Mick a question it involved something concerning Missey. As Twyla sat there in the wing chair, I wondered what she saw in a man old enough to be a father-and-a-half. She started caressing a ring on her left hand that held a stone the size of a Greenland iceberg. That ended my speculation.

Mick wanted to show Twyla the ocean. She decided to put on her bathing suit at the house in case there was no place to change at the beach. The girl proved to have acute sewing abilities. You'd have been impressed to see the way she had created a bathing suit out of two corn plasters and a Band-Aid. Her stomach was as flat as Saskatchewan. I thought back to the day when, in a fit of shopper's optimism, I tried on one of those two-piece bathing suits. The part of me that was supposed to resemble Saskatchewan looked more like the foothills of Alberta.

Twyla twisted her hair into a ponytail and pulled it through a hole at the back of a baseball cap. As she bobbed along the beach holding Mick's hand she looked like a young filly itching for her first race. Somehow we got through the afternoon, and I think that Mick was as relieved as we were when it was time for them to leave.

As they walked out the lane toward the red Ferrari, Twyla, ponytail bobbing, slipped her hand into Mick's and began to skip. At that moment it seemed that Mick's step became lighter too. "I don't understand it," I said as I watched them. "Mick seems so...so..."

"Happy?" whispered my husband over my shoulder.

Yes, darn it, Mick was happy. In fact, in all the years we had known him, I had never seen him look, talk, or act the way he did that afternoon. And then I thought about Missey and the last time we had lunch together. She was relaxed and smiling. She had just redecorated her oceanfront condo and confided that she was "seeing" someone.

I turned from the window, pulled a can of Lysol out of the cupboard, and began to spray everything the two of them had touched, giving the wing chair an extra shot of disinfectant.

"Why are you doing that?" my husband asked.

"When it comes to TYW," I said, "one can't be too careful."

THE DIRECTIONAL DYSFUNCTION OF CANADIANS

While driving across Canada, never, ever, leave the Trans Canada Highway because no one knows how to get back on it again.

I finally realized why men don't ask for directions. There's no point to it, because even when you ask, nobody can tell you anything. This realization surfaced on a motorcycle trip across western Canada from Calgary to Winnipeg. We had spent the night in Regina and were looking for something called the Ring Road. Certainly, even for an unseasoned traveller, the name "Ring Road" implies a highway running in a circular direction around the edge of the city, allowing motorists to travel from one side of it to the other without encountering local traffic. Simple. That is, if you can find the Ring Road. When we ended up in an obscure subdivision on a street that appeared to be turning into a cow path, we stopped and asked a woman how to get to the Ring Road. She smiled and said, "I guess we Regina people are a little confusing." She kindly offered to lead us to the Ring Road while we followed her. Regina people are also very kind.

It was in a restaurant in Portage la Prairie when we summoned up the courage to try asking for directions again. Our waitress was Jan, a middle aged woman with hair the colour of autumn grain. She was pleasant and helpful, that is, until we asked a silly question. "What's the quickest way to get back on the Trans Canada Highway?" Have you ever watched what happens to a person when they are asked a question like that?

Jan's face did a meltdown. Her expression followed a progression - from blankness, to confusion, to absolute pain. She pointed to a balding middle-aged man who was serving a table in the next section of the restaurant and muttered, "I'll ask Boyd. He's the expert around here." It soon became obvious that Boyd's directional senses had atrophied, so much so that he never did find his way to our table.

We somehow made it to Winnipeg where we had an enjoyable week with family and friends. On the return trip to Calgary we decided to see some more of the country, so we headed north on the Yellowhead Highway to Saskatoon and Lloydminster. This might have been a good idea if we hadn't left the Yellowhead to drive into Saskatoon for gas. Inside the gas bar there was a little coffee shop. The girl behind the counter looked to be about seventeen but she would reach the drinking age by the time we left, all because of a simple question: "How do we get back on the highway to Lloydminster?" From that moment on we entered a time warp - we ceased to exist.

"Hey, Marty," she called to a young man coming in the side door, "How do you get to Lloyd?" Marty appeared to need counsel, for the next second he turned to the man behind him and they began to deliberate on the problem of getting to Lloyd. The girl began waiting on the next customer, ignoring us completely. I knew then that none of these people had ever *left* Saskatoon. I also began to harbour a fear that *we* would never leave Saskatoon. This is the only reason we have settlement on the Canadian prairie. No one has ever figured out a way to leave. There's only one thing to do when you are being completely ignored. Go quietly.

"Let's just turn left at that light on the corner and keep driving north," I suggested as we walked to our Goldwing. It worked. We got to Lloyd in time for supper. I realized then why the people back in Saskatoon had been nonplussed by our request for directions. The city of Lloydminster straddles the Alberta\Saskatchewan border. Of course, we should have been more specific. They hadn't known whether we wanted to go to Lloydminster, **Saskatchewan** or Lloydminster, **Alberta**.

The only place where directional dysfunction does not appear to exist is Vegreville, Alberta. That's because Vegreville is actually a training ground for civil engineers. You can drive into Vegreville, right past their big pasanka (actually, the largest in the world), buy gas,

65

stop for coffee, and then you just keep on driving. Eventually you come back out on the Yellowhead Highway again. Yes, Vegreville is a city that is easy to love.

Lest you think that directional dysfunction is an affliction specific to the prairies, I would advise you that it is a nation-wide problem. Canadians simply don't believe in signs. It appears to stem from a red light mentality; you know, the need for a red light every fifty feet. When you are required to stop that often who has time to go anywhere? Let me tell you about a case in British Columbia.

Several years ago on Vancouver Island, the highway leading to the Swartz Bay ferry terminal was upgraded and a new overpass was built. Unfortunately, directional signs to accompany the new changes were not only sparse, but confusing.

One day I was flagged down on the overpass by a carload of tourists from Texas. The driver of the car pointed to the ferry terminal where the Queen of Vancouver was docked, a perfect picture of tranquillity. "Ma'am, can you tell me how to get to that there boat?" asked the Texan, his face the colour of a Sidney summer sunrise. "Sure," I said, "go to the next stop light and turn left. That will put you on the four-lane highway going south – the one you see below. Now, it may look as though you're going in the wrong direction, and actually you are. But when you get to the first light, turn right. Then immediately make a U-turn and come back to the light. If the light ever turns green, hang a left. This will put you back on the road to the ferry terminal – that one down there," I said, pointing to the highway below us. "Actually, that's our Trans-Canada Highway. You can't miss it."

As the Texan surveyed me with an expression of disbelief, I longed to tell him about the engineers in Vegreville.

AN ATTACK OF ROAD RAGE CAN LEAD TO AN ATTACK BY A KILLER BURRITO

What is it that comes over human beings when they are confined to 400 cubic feet of space surrounded by steel, glass and chrome? You can take the most benign, tractable driver in the world and ten minutes after putting him in a vehicle and turning him loose on a highway, he qualifies for a career in contract killing.

It is only a matter of time until some other driver cuts him off or tailgates or drives too slowly in the passing lane. And then, it happens. With a face twisted like the slinky from last Christmas, his mouth becomes a launch pad for obscenities, while a solitary middle finger rises in a universal salute that requires no interpretation. It is a full-blown case of Road Rage.

Actually, road rage is nothing new. It has been with us since the first man jumped into a wheeled vehicle. I think it started with the Romans. If you have any doubt, rent the movie *Ben Hur* and watch the chariot race between Charlton Heston and the evil character named Messala. This case of road rage ended in the death of Messala.

Even today, when everyone is supposed to be more civilized than those pugnacious Romans, road rage can end in death, or, at the very least, personal injury. Take the case of Daryl and Edward, two grown men past middle age. Old enough to know better. One lazy Saturday when Edward was driving home from an Old Timers' hockey game, he decided to stop at Tim Horton's for some TimBits. As he pulled out of Tim Horton's parking lot, his 1965 Volkswagon van collided with a Hummer driven by Daryl, who had just left TacoTime. Edward and Daryl jumped out of their vehicles and engaged in a little chest butting, like a couple of Rocky Mountain Big Horned sheep.

The important thing to know about this accident is that Daryl was eating a burrito. Now, eating a burrito is not dangerous in its own right, but when the burrito is being eaten by a person who is butting his chest and waving his arms around, it can take on the momentum of a launched nuclear warhead. Somehow, the burrito ended up between Edward's lips with such force that it knocked one of his teeth loose. Daryl claimed it was an accident and refused to accept responsibility for the burrito injury. However, Edward decided to sue for damages.

It proved to be a difficult case for Judge Keepin who dreaded the idea of his name being entered in the law books under "The Burrito Assault Case."

Edward's lawyer maintained that Daryl was in peaceable possession of the burrito at the time of attack and that possession is nine-tenths of the law. Daryl's lawyer claimed that the burrito had left Daryl's hand, which meant it was no longer Daryl's responsibility. In essence, the burrito acted under its own power and must be charged separately under the "Dangerous Goods and Noxious Things" section" of the Criminal Code.

Witnesses proved unreliable. One man who had stopped at the intersection said he thought it wasn't a burrito but an enchilada that had jumped all over Edward, and a middle-aged woman was positive the thing had hit Edward in the eye, not the mouth. A young jogger who took the stand couldn't remember whether Daryl had struck Edward with the burrito or if it was Edward who had laid it on to Daryl. Then a teenager testified that Daryl had said, "Take that, you measly little jerk!" while an elderly man swore he heard, "Take that, you jeezley little clerk!" (The only relevant fact to be gained from this testimony was that, because of the use of the word "jeezley," it was obvious the elderly man had come from New Brunswick.)

Finally, after both lawyers had rested their cases under the Bench, Judge Keepin asked for a recess. Judge Keepin was well known for his extended recesses. In this instance, the recess was so long that to date the case is still unresolved. Since then, Daryl has undergone bypass surgery and now follows a burrito-free diet and Edward, in keeping with his toothless image, signed up for an old timers hockey team called the Hot Peppers. The burrito remains under lock and key as "Exhibit 1" in the RCMP locker, that is, unless some constable doing the night shift has run out of Tim Horton doughnuts and eaten it. The lawyers are still counting their money.

SEX ON THE TSAWWASSEN RUN

Perhaps on previous ferry crossings between Vancouver and Vancouver Island I had been too preoccupied with the scenery or my book or the cafeteria to notice; however, one day it dawned on me. Sex is booming on the Tsawwassen run.

We were sitting in the front salon, on the side near the window. Three rows ahead of us a young couple sat gazing into each other's eyes. They may as well have been on a slow boat to China for all they cared. The girl was caressing the back of her sweetheart's neck with long delicate fingers, curling them sensuously around his ear lobes. A few seconds later they were locked in a kiss that defied the laws of physics. It appeared they were rehearsing for an x-rated movie. Perhaps someone should tell them that this was a PG ferry.

Or was it? After ten minutes had elapsed and neither one had come up for air, I turned my attention to a middle-aged couple coming down the aisle. I couldn't discern whether the t-shirts they wore were testament to their age, occupation, or sexual prowess.

"Do it in cement. It stays up longer," was the male's announcement in bold black letters stretching across a rock-hard chest. His partner, in bleached and acid-washed jeans that had obviously shrunk in the dryer, hooked one arm lovingly through his. The words undulating over the uneven terrain of her bosom were, "Forty and foxy." This pair must be dynamite!

Curious now to see what else was enfolding on my B.C. "love boat", I began observing a well-read family of four in the row ahead of me. The daughter, about thirteen, was bent over an article in a teen magazine entitled, "The First Time He Asks - 'Yes' Or 'No'?" The father, balding, pale and paunchy, was oblivious to all around him.

His topic of interest was, "Men's Sexual Fantasies - Say Goodbye to Guilt." Perhaps if he had been able to bring himself back to the real world for a minute he might have noticed his wife was ingesting an article entitled, "Should You Have An Affair?" Ah, well, at least their teenaged son was holding up the family's moral code. He was immersed in a copy of "Car and Cycle." But wait a minute. Closer inspection revealed a bare-breasted woman in tight leather pants sprawled across a motorcycle. At least he wasn't biting his lip like Dad; nor was his brow pressed into a frown like Mom's. There were no decisions to make here. Only pure, unmitigated pleasure.

What if, at that moment, they had all traded magazines? What might happen? A trip to the marriage counsellor? Birds-and-bees discussions? Family communication?

I cast a glance back at the young couple who had been scuba-kissing. It was only a matter of time...

As I turned to share my observations with my partner, I found him surveying a pretty young blonde in a pair of shorts that were little more than an apology. There was only one thing left to do. I reached into my purse and pulled out my book, "Passion at Peeley Point."

DIETS CAN LEAD TO LOSS OF LIFE

There is in life a moment of truth. It comes in the doctor's office when he pulls you aside and advises that you have been exceeding the feed limit. Suddenly what pops into your mind is an obscene, four-letter word. DIET!

It seems that anyone over the age of twelve has tried some kind of diet. But diets can lead to loss of life. Remember Scarsdale? It took four hours to prepare a meal and four seconds to inhale it. Four minutes later you were starving. One day my husband and I sat down to one of those Scarsdale concoctions and I started to say, "Now, you have to remember to eat slow..." He glowered at me like a ferret in a gopher hole and snarled through his lettuce, "I'll eat any way I darn well please!" (He didn't really say "darn".) Yes, Virginia, there was definitely homicide in the air. The only question that remained was which one of us would do the other in first?

Then there was the grapefruit diet I tried after the birth of my third child. After one week of grapefruit, tomatoes and boiled eggs I baked up a batch of chocolate chip cookies and ate them all before the oven had cooled down.

I discovered that every time we started on a new diet my husband took calorie books to bed. As I endeavoured to concentrate on a copy of War *and Peace* or *A Brief History of Time*, he would read aloud to me the number of calories in a tablespoon of butter or a two-inch porterhouse steak. As I said, diets can lead to loss of life.

A certain elder in our family used to maintain there was only one sure way to lose weight: the "pushing away from the table" diet. This, you understand, was from a man who spouted such gems of wisdom as, "water seeks its own level," "there's no drinking in a bottle of whisky," and (after a car accident), "the sonofagun just came out of nowhere." (He didn't say "sonofagun" either.)

I have to admit that his idea has merit. But self-discipline isn't enough. Pushing away from that last scoop of mashed potatoes and gravy, that second piece of apple pie, will require a little help. I think I have the answer. Not only will it solve the "push away" problem, it will do wonders for the environment.

Remember all those abdominizers that were sold years ago to firm up your tummy? I understand a great many of them have ended up in landfill sites. I think with some minor adjustments they could be just what the "push away" followers need. You know how those contraptions work like a rocking chair? Well, you could sit inside one and rock back and forth between the table and the chair. On every rock forward, you spoon in a mouthful of pie. But then when you rock away, no pie. You end up eating half the amount you normally eat, acquiring some great abs in the process. Maybe we could re-name this the "Abdominizer Diet."

There is one sure way of losing weight. Go and visit your children - the ones who have left home and are now buying their own groceries. This could be called the "Empty Nest Diet." For breakfast you will receive only black coffee (that is, provided they have remembered to *buy* coffee). Lunch may well be the same unless you take the initiative and buy a loaf of bread and something to put between the slices. They may make something for dinner but chances are you will eat out, whereby you end up eating the smallest thing on the menu because you are the one paying the check. Any calories you consume on this diet will likely come from the beer in their refrigerator, which is always in ample supply. After two days you will have lost ten pounds. After two weeks your lawyer will be probating your will, proving once again that diets can lead to loss of life.

Those of us who ride the eating/dieting merry-go-round are sometimes at a loss to remember who we are and where we stand in the grand scheme of things. A few summers ago, I attended a 4-H exhibition of steer and heifer calves that had been raised by young people from a farming community. As the judges walked around each animal to inspect it, they kept poking and prodding it in various places. I asked a rancher sitting beside me to explain what was going on. "Well," he said, shifting the lump of Beechnut from his left to his right cheek, "if you push your fingers into a calf and the meat feels firm, it is considered fat enough to be "finished." On the other hand, if the flesh feels soft, the animal is "not ready." As I listened carefully to the cattleman, I surreptitiously slipped a hand under my t-shirt and pressed my fingers into those parts that protruded, like leavening dinner rolls, over cloth and elastic boundaries. Suddenly it all became clear to me, a revelation of my special place in the world of weight-watching. I felt a profound sense of peace as I was finally able to put a label on my physical uniqueness. Finished.

Somewhere between having a waist like a wasp and a backside like a bumblebee, there has to be a happy medium.

BE KIND TO ORANGE PYLONS - YOU
NEVER KNOW
WHERE YOU'LL MEET ONE

If you've ever tried to drive across this nation during the summer you've run into them - road construction crews. A typical road construction crew consists of a million bright orange pylons, enough massive equipment to overrun Baghdad, and a flag person. There is also one guy in a pickup who always seems to be driving somewhere, and someone in a giant dump truck that is continually backing up while making loud beeping sounds. At the side of the road you will usually find four workers standing on an asphalt spreader, one on each corner, and they appear to be waiting - either for the guy in the pickup to tell them what to do or for the person in the dump truck to finish backing up.

This, of course, is assuming you come across the construction site when the crew is not having their coffee break or eating their lunch. During this hallowed time the only physical movement is performed by the flag person, the cute little female holding the big STOP sign. There is tremendous power in this position. A simple flick of the wrist and she is able to hold up traffic all the way from Moose Jaw to Halifax. Sometimes she raises the STOP sign even when there appears no need to stop. However, this is absolutely necessary to allow the dump truck to continue backing up and clear a path for the guy in the pickup. It also provides protection for the four people on the asphalt spreader who are halfway through their peanut butter sandwiches.

Some construction projects are carried out by replacing highway workers with orange pylons. Last summer we drove nineteen miles on the Trans Canada Highway, weaving in and out of orange pylons like an Olympic skier going for a gold medal, and never saw one dump truck, pickup, or asphalt spreader. In place of the flag person there was a big red sign: SLOW. ROAD CONSTRUCTION FOR NEXT NINETEEN MILES. Actually, orange pylons may be the way of the future for many things. There is every indication that they may one day replace bank tellers, Hudson's Bay clerks, and doctors. Sometimes it appears the transition has already been made. Like the last time I tried to find a clerk in the Bay's china department. As my pleas for help in the wilderness of Royal Albert and Noritake echoed off the walls, even the appearance of a single orange pylon would have been a comfort.

But wait, how did I arrive here, wandering in the deserted china department of The Bay looking for a clerk? Before that I had been driving along the Trans Canada Highway looking for any human beings who might be working on the road.

It has long been suspected that most of our road construction is performed at night, which is why you don't see anyone actually working during the daylight hours. It's much cooler then and there is less traffic on the highway for the flagperson to stop. Also, the workers don't need as many lunch breaks, although coffee is still a big factor in keeping everyone awake until morning.

But I want to get back to the guy in the pickup who is always driving somewhere. Have you ever found yourself stuck behind one of these icons as they head back into town? It is possible to run faster than they drive. People have been known to age five weeks simply by following one of these pickups for five miles, particularly between the hours of 2:00 to 3:30 in the afternoon. The calculated top speed is two miles per hour because, you understand, it is only two miles back to the government garage, and if the pickup driver was to return before quitting time it might throw the whole outfit into a state of disarray. So this is why the guy in the pickup is always driving. He is never **supposed** to get anywhere.

There is a story about a group of tourists standing at the edge of the Grand Canyon. The tour guide says, "It took five million years for this canyon to be created." One of the tourists responds, "I never knew it was a government project." Obviously the tourist had at some point encountered a road construction crew.

MEXICAN BEER AND SHIP TIME

It was while we were celebrating twenty-five years of Marriage Survival with a Caribbean cruise that we ran into her. You know the type, the tourist who has been everywhere and done everything and goes on subsequent tours for one purpose only: to astound others with all of their accumulated knowledge. This particular day it was Ms. Profound, one of forty bus passengers headed for the Mayan ruins outside Cozumel, Mexico under the guidance of a cheery little Mexican named Manuel.

Ms. Profound sat across the aisle from us, note pad in hand, a beaming smile on her face, and wrote everything down that Manuel said, even the sentence, "Thees ees the best dreenk in the uneeverse," as he passed around bottles of cold Mexican beer. To further enhance her presence, Ms. Profound wore a hat; not an ordinary sun visor type or even a floppy Tilley-style, but one with a brim wide enough to shade an entire baseball park. And its straw edges had frayed, giving it a serrated look. As Manuel pointed to things of interest out the bus windows, she kept turning her head from one side to the other, all the while grinning and scribbling in her notebook. A clockwise spin of her hat left a saw cut in the forehead of the man behind her; a counter-clockwise spin and the woman in the seat beside her lost part of her scalp.

A half-hour drive put us at the edge of the ruins. We followed Manuel through the leaves to a little stone house with a rectangular door. As we huddled around him, giving a wide berth to Ms. Profound, he told us about the stone path leading to the altar where virgins had been sacrificed to the gods. Then he made the mistake of asking if there were any questions. It was the moment she had been waiting for. There followed a barrage of queries preceded by a great waving of her wrist and a reiteration of our guide's name. For instance: "Manuel. Oh, Manuel. Is it true that before the young women were sacrificed they were smeared in extra virgin olive oil?" or "Manuel. Oh, Manuel. Isn't it a fact that when King Wompoopus was told that his people were starving, he said, 'Let them eat snake'?"

Manuel was beginning to ignore her and so were we. We sauntered off on our own to investigate the stone path leading to the altar. It was an eerie place. The dry leaves rustled under our feet and the air felt oppressive, as though filled with the ancient spirits of the dead. I imagined myself as a young Mayan girl, smeared in extra virgin olive oil, making that walk up the stone path toward my fate with the question running through my mind, "I wonder, did I turn off the stove?"

Just then an iguana the size of a Newfoundland dog dropped out of a tree into the leaves only twenty feet from where I was standing. I have to hand it to our little tour guide. When he heard me cry, "Manuel. Oh, Manuel!" he acted quickly. It only took him an hour to get me out of that tree, with the assurance that, "Eet ees only a leetle leezard."

After he had led me back to the bus and cracked open another case of Mexican beer, the trauma diminished - somewhat. Our next stop was a white sandy beach where we hoped to do some snorkelling. Now, there is a cardinal rule of cruise ships. To avoid confusion, they insist that passengers maintain their watches on ship time. Manuel, being a responsible tour guide, wanted to remind us of this. He pointed to his watch. "Remember," he said, we must get you to your sh-e-e-p on time. Please check your watches now. You need to be back here at the bus at three o'clock sh-e-e-p time. Remember, three o'clock sh-e-e-p time."

I guess it was bound to happen. Some things can only go so far. There was a flurry across the aisle as Ms. Profound waved her wrist. "Manuel. Oh, Manuel!" Our little guide finally acknowledged her, no doubt in fear that her hand might snap off and go careening through the bus like a rocket-launched grenade. "Yes?" he said, not really looking at her. And then, notebook in hand, pen poised above it, she asked, "Manuel. What is sheep time?"

It's funny how at that very moment no one in the bus had been speaking. Her question hung there, like a barbecued duck in the window of a Chinese grocery store. Then came the laughter - not polite little titters or discreet snickers but loud, unmitigated guffaws, especially from the man with the saw-cut wound and the woman who was missing the large swatch of hair. Yes, somewhere out there in the universe there exists a goddess of justice. At least that is the case in Cozumel, Mexico.

Most days I operate on sheep time.

WILL I EVER GO ACROSS THE SEA TO IRELAND?

For years I've been trying to get to Ireland. My reasons are many: I have Irish roots, I have corresponded with an Irish woman named Kathleen for twenty-five years and only seen her in photographs, and I have this deep-seated urge to sit in an Irish pub, swinging my glass back and forth, and sing Irish songs. The most pressing reason, however, is this. Ever since I heard the *Kingston Trio* sing about "the Mountains of Mourne," I have felt another deep-seated urge: to wander in their midst. This was further reinforced by a little story told to me by my friend, Jim, a native Irishman. "We used to have a saying. If you looked toward the Mountains of Mourne and couldn't see them, it was raining. If you *could* see them, it was *going* to rain."

Three years ago, when my last child moved out, I felt the Irish blood beginning to stir in my veins. I knew my dream was starting to materialize. I made up a special file marked "Ireland" and put into it every scrap of information I could find. An evening of surfing the Internet provided an address for Northern Ireland Tourism. I could literally feel the mist from the Mountains of Mourne on my cheeks as I devoured the seventeen pounds of information they sent me. I bought six tapes of Irish music and each time Paddy Ryan sang "Danny Boy" I fairly died of homesickness. In fact, I was so sure that I was finally going to see my Emerald Isle that in my "Across the Miles" Christmas card to Kathleen, I wrote "See you in '95."

Children, left to their natural evolvement, will marry, which is what happened the following spring. At the end of May I was too exhausted to wander through the Mountains of Mourne. The only "emerald aisle" I saw that year was the green stretch of lawn under my feet as I walked beside the groomsman to the front of the wedding party as mother of the bride. By November, however, I had fully recovered and my Irish blood was surging anew. With "The Rose Of Tralee" playing on the stereo and a picture of Kathleen above my typewriter, I wrote in my "Across the Miles" Christmas message, "See you in '96." Irish women are very patient.

The wedding of '95 must have precipitated some kind of nuptial contagion because in '96 there were two more weddings in the family. After return trips to Alberta in "high season" and the purchase of two wedding gifts we suddenly had a new focus - paying off our credit card. I could feel the mist on my cheeks beginning to evaporate.

Would I never set foot on the sod that my great grandfather had set foot on when he left that country? Was my pub dream limited to swinging a mason jar of beer in front of the stereo while Foster & Allen sang, "If We Had Old Ireland Here"? Would Kathleen forever be only a Kodak moment?

But as I said, I have Irish roots. We don't give up without a fight. Did I lapse into resignation, content to see the Mountains of Mourne from an armchair? Not on your life! As I wrote "See you in '97" in my "Across the Miles" Christmas message to Kathleen, I pondered the wisdom of purchasing a date stamp. That way I could simply roll up a new year each time, although I understand that after 1999 I might run into a problem.

1997 dawned with new hope. With the whole family married off, I watched my "Riverdance" video for the seventeenth time, and my Irish eyes fairly glistened with anticipation. But I had overlooked the economic cleansing which takes place in this country every April. After Revenue Canada had taken its 2.24 kg. of personal DNA and three-quarters of my savings, I barely had enough money left to buy a tape entitled "Irish Echoes." The mist on my cheeks had taken a new form: little salty tears of disillusionment.

Not for long, however. At the end of October I created a Christmas card on my new computer. On the front was a picture of a maple leaf under the caption "Across the Miles." Inside I placed a picture of a leprechaun holding a mug of beer, along with these words: "I'm Writing You From Home Again, Kathleen. See you in '98."

As of 2006 I have still not made it Ireland. I now carry a spray bottle filled with Irish Mist.

THE HORRIBLE PART OF SEXY MOVIES –
ENDING UP IN THE SAME GRAVY BOAT

It seems the biggest box office movies are the ones that either scare the wits out of you or charm your pants off. Horror and sex: the two subjects most able to make us forget our own lives for a couple of hours.

But let's face it. Scary movies are so...predictable. The victim, when chased by an attacker bent on sending them to the next dimension, always runs up or down a set of steps. Either up a seemingly endless staircase, or down into a basement where there are twenty-seven objects to hide behind. No one ever thinks of running outside where it is safe. Actually, actors spend half their lives running up and down stairs, which is why they never gain any weight.

I watched a movie many years ago where a woman was lying in bed in her sexy white lingerie and she heard someone coming up the stairs - one step at a time. What did she do? Did she open the bedroom window and scream her lungs out? Did she jump down into the lilac bush to safety? No, she just lay there, breathing heavily, her eyes as big as dinner plates, while the intruder came closer - one step at a time, while we in the audience chewed on our nails and wondered, "Why doesn't he do this in his stocking feet?"

Stairs played a big part in creating suspense each time Bette Davis went up to check on her prisoner, Joan Crawford in the movie *Whatever Happened to Baby Jane?* The stairway exaggerated the feeling of entrapment and terror, not to mention the intensity of nail-biting in the audience.

In *Presumed Innocent*, we find Harrison Ford, trotting down a spider-web infested set of steps into the basement, where he discovers an object that reveals a horrible truth. (It turns out to be a dust mop, which proves that no one in the Sabbich household gives a frosty grape about housecleaning.)

If horror relies on stairs for its effect, certainly sex relies on the use of water. Actors, when they are not running up and down stairs, are usually writhing around in wet clothing that clings to the skin, trying to titillate our psyche.

Some of you may remember the television mini-series, *Thorn Birds*, in which Richard Chamberlain comes trudging up the long, deserted beach toward Meggie, the love of his life. Meggie starts trudging down the long, deserted beach toward him, the love of *her* life. After enough time has elapsed for you to defrost your freezer, they meet and grapple and eventually fall down, dousing their hot libidos in the ocean. This little roll in the surf resulted in Meggie becoming pregnant.

Then again, there is Harrison Ford, all wet on a deserted island with Evelyn deGeneres, in the movie, *Six Days and Seven Nights*. (No wonder he is one of the biggest box-office draws of all time. He has the ability to be both sexy AND horrible.)

As most of you know, water, mixed with dirt, turns to mud. Think back to the movie *Ghost*. This production may have been the result of the producer and director attending a mud-wrestling match. Remember that sexy scene between Patrick Swayze and Demi Moore in front of her potter's wheel? After he puts his hands on her bowl, it's only a matter of time until they both end up covered in mud. The intrigue lies in wondering if they will eventually end up in the same gravy boat. Now that's sexy!

Perhaps we non-celebrities should look closer at the movie industry and the potential benefits of trying the "water experience" at home. Think about it. One night you pop into the shower with all your clothes on and then, as you stand there at the bedroom door, shivering and dripping all over the carpet, your lover looks up from the latest copy of *Sports Illustrated* and says, "Are you crazy? You're going to catch your death of cold!"

No, I think the water approach only works in the fantasy world of movies, where no one ever catches cold or has the flu. I would certainly never try it, not with my aversion to stepping into water deeper than my ankles. But then, I've never met Harrison Ford on a deserted beach.

A COLD, HARD LOOK CAN LEAD TO SOMETHING COSY

When was the last time you met a travelling Swede? Think about it. Have you ever run into one of those young world travellers laden down like an alpaca who said, "Ja, I vas yust going around da vorld"?

The truth is, Swedes don't travel. It's because they have more fun at home. You see, Sweden is one of the most sexually liberated countries in the world. It probably started with something simple, like trying to keep warm.

But what about other countries? Germany, for example. It's a well-known fact that Germans love to travel - and do. In fact, in a survey done some years ago it was discovered that German men would rather drive their cars than have sex. It was also discovered that the most-often repeated expression to be heard from German women is: "Well, go right ahead, then. Just remember, *I'm* the one with the Volvo!"

Let's investigate this phenomenon a little closer to home. Take a look at Newfoundland. Another survey has concluded that Newfoundlanders have more sex than the rest of Canadians. Take this a step further and ask yourself, "When was the last time you met a travelling Newfie?" *"Yes, bye, I was just comin' where you're at to see how you be."* It would appear that, once again, the hypothesis is: The more sex, the more reason to stay home.

Of course, some economists would disagree with this altogether. They might speculate that the real reason Swedes don't travel is due to their high taxation rate. With Sweden's highly socialized system of government, there is simply no money left for travelling outside the country. But we could challenge those same economists with the fact that even though Canada is one of the most highly taxed countries in the world, its residents still leave the country - in droves: young people, searching for a country where they will have more after-tax dollars in their GWG jeans, and old people, searching for a country where snow is only a memory. Unlike the Swedes who simply hunker down with their significant other, older Canadians actually evolve into another species - Snowbirds.

Some of you may be wondering what all this has to do with sex. Nothing. Snowbirds don't spend that much time in bed. They are too busy golfing in Florida, hiking in Arizona, or swimming in Hawaii, to engage in a pursuit that consumed so much of their time when they were young and cold and overtaxed. They are still overtaxed, of course, but the golfing and hiking and swimming help them to forget.

In survey after survey, it appears that sex has become a kind of common denominator by which we measure the state of contentment of individuals, provinces, countries. But the sexual act can also serve as an anodyne for those who are not only cold, but distressed. There is the story of a tobacco farmer in southwestern Ontario who had come from one of the Carolinas. One morning he went out to survey his tobacco fields and discovered the entire crop had turned black from frost. He trudged back into the bedroom, climbed into bed, and reached for his partner with the words, "Honey, this is all we got."

So, is it cold weather, after all, that produces the intriguing statistics put out by all these sexual surveys, the ones which seem to be performed on a weekly basis? I think your best bet is to ask a Swede or a Newfoundlander - if you ever run into one.

COMPUTER RELATIONSHIPS

Sometimes a person simply has to accept the forces of change and get on with their life. That's what happened when I decided to buy my first computer. It wasn't an easy decision, not after everything I had heard about the temperamental nature of these machines - entire manuscripts being wiped out in an instant, computers that talked back or refused to shut down even after you pulled the plug. Was I ready for a commitment like this? I had to try. Yes, if I wanted to move forward, I had to put an end to my typewriter relationship. On Sept. 4, 1996 I took the plunge.

I have lived long enough to know that in any relationship, attitude is the key. Like a new bride, I made up my mind that, despite all I had heard, *my* computer relationship would be different. I also knew that sometimes even a successful relationship needs outside professional help. I contacted Hugh. What Hugh doesn't know about computers is still waiting to be discovered. Not only was he able to untangle all the wires, plugs and cables that came in the box and connect them to their proper slots and spots, he proved to be a kind and patient teacher. That was obvious right away. When he asked me where I would like to start and I answered, "Can you show me how to turn it on?" Hugh simply smiled.

Another thing I appreciated about Hugh was the fact that he always brought along a pointer. I am one of the pointer-generation, from a time when teachers used such things to indicate facts and figures on a blackboard, to tap desks in an effort to regain our attention, and sometimes to whack us over the back when we forgot the dates of important events, such as the day, month and year that Laura Secord started making chocolates. (Hugh would NEVER tap or whack!)

Hugh and I sat down in front of this array of technology spread across my new computer table, and then he said something important. "Just remember. You can't break it." All of my computer anxiety evaporated like a pre-election promise.

I learned quickly and Mr. Pentium and I got along well. In fact, I began to wonder how I had ever had a life without him. I was feeling rather proud of myself until one evening about a month later. I made the big mistake of involving a third party - another man. It started innocently enough. My husband and I were sitting around sipping on a glass of cabernet when I said, "Wanta play an Encarta game?" Probably because of the cabernet, he agreed. Using a chopstick for a pointer, I shared with him everything I had learned, like how to turn the computer on and where to click on the "x," and then I let him have the mouse.

For a good half-hour he wandered through various rooms in a stone castle, answering history questions. A correct answer allowed him to proceed to the next room; an incorrect one brought an ignorant sound from Mr. Pentium. Since my husband is very good at history, he advanced quickly.

I don't know what happened next. Perhaps he got tired, or maybe he right-clicked on the door to the left or left-clicked on the door to the right. Whatever it was, he couldn't get out of the room. There ensued a claustrophobic attempt to escape. Sweat appeared on his upper lip, glistening in the light from the monitor, and he was clicking the mouse so fast it sounded like Michael Flattley on amphetamines. I could only watch in helplessness.

What to do? It was nearly midnight, much too late to call Hugh. Were we doomed to spend the rest of the night imprisoned inside a castle room, somewhere in cyberspace? Suddenly, as mysteriously as we had become trapped, we moved to another room. There must be a fairy godmother in the land of Encarta. A tooth fairy at least. On the top left of the screen there was a button marked "Home." "Click on it!" I screamed, pointing with my chopstick.

It worked. We were FREE, FREE AT LAST! My husband rose from the chair, muttering something about Mr. Pentium being descended from a canine. Quickly, I shut the computer down, collapsing in a heap across the keyboard, with the realization that I should have followed the advice of an old adage: "Two's company. Three's a crowd."

* *These days I practice computer monogamy*

WHEN WE CAN GROW OUR OWN
BODY PARTS
WE'LL HAVE IT ALL TOGETHER

Remember when you were a kid with knees like trampolines and you could jump over fences, candlesticks and tall buildings with a single bound? Now your knees have all the elasticity of petrified wood and when you jump over a crack in the sidewalk they make a crunching sound that can be heard all the way to Ellesmere Island. The problem is mice. Let me explain.

The surface of the two bones that make up the knee joint (the femur and the tibia) is covered with a substance called linoleum. It's actually a layer of no-wax, cushion-floor cartilage and it provides for a smooth encounter between the bones during strenuous movement, such as walking to the refrigerator. Unfortunately, over time, this linoleum gets all chewed up much like the floor tiles in your mud room. The little pieces that break off and float around inside the knee have been given a highly scientific medical designation: "joint mice."

The name arose when a young doctor was examining the knee of a patient named Jack who had jumped over a candlestick. As she held her stethoscope close to Jack's damaged knee, she heard these words, "What's a cute little mouse like you doing in a joint like this?" This story was recently reported in an issue of the *Physicians and Surgeons Journal of Preposterous Prognostications.*

The favoured method of eradicating joint mice is not by trap or poison. A substance is used that is completely harmless and toxin free, i.e. water. A doctor immobilizes the patient's knee between two medical journals and inserts two tiny holes in the area with a crochet hook. With a sprayer head attached to a garden hose she can now blast all those little mice to that Great Knee Joint In The Sky. Afterwards the patient is able to walk to the refrigerator with no problem at all.

Actually, with all the wonders of modern science, it won't be long until we are able to grow our own replacement body parts. Don't scoff. Anything is possible. Remember the first time someone told you it was possible to send pictures through the air and project them onto a screen in your living room, and you didn't believe it? Do you believe in t.v. now? And whoever thought they would be able to sit in their office in Tuktoyaktuk, north of the 53rd, and listen to a radio station in Moscow, also north of the 53rd, by means of something called the Internet. Also, don't forget that Scottish piece of fleece named Dolly who was cloned from an udder - excuse me, *other* - sheep.

To grow your own body parts all you will need is a petrie dish, some cell nutrients and a DNA probe. Your doctor can insert the probe into whichever body part you want to replace and extract a couple of DNA threads which she then puts into a plastic bag of liquid nutrients and seals with a twist tie. If you've ever carried goldfish home from the pet store you should be able to handle this with no problem. Once you are home, simply transfer everything to a petrie dish, cover and store in a cool place. You will have to add nutrients periodically but don't overfeed. Remember what happened when you overfed the goldfish.

Can you imagine the competition among multi-national firms for a share of the nutrient market for home-grown body parts? It will be fierce and ruthless. In addition to newspaper ads and t.v. commercials that promote products for every body part that weeps or seeps, we will be bombarded at least twenty-seven times during the six o'clock news or the "Red Green Show" with promises such as:

"Double your bra size with Dr. Knocker's Miracle Gel."
"Thumbuddies, all you'll ever need for healthy thumbs."
"Liven up your liver with Carter's Little Liver Pills." (Wait a minute. I think this one has already been done.)

Growing your own body parts will provide a sense of control over your future medical welfare. It will also insure that you do not burden the Canadian Medicare System with your need for medical attention. Not to mention the money it will save, considering that the cost of removing and transporting donor organs is more than a full tank of gasoline.

You may even decide to grow some spare parts for those members of your family who are either too busy to grow their own or the ones who don't have a flesh-coloured thumb. But that, of course, will depend on how well you get along with your family and which ones you deem worthy of life extension.

To have, once again, two knees that work like trampolines - that's a day worth waiting for. Then it's no time until we'll be leaping over fences, candlesticks and tall buildings with a single bound. Even in Ellesmere Island.

THE FINANCIAL SPINOFFS OF
BULLET-RIDDEN SHIRTS
AND ROYAL TEDDY BEARS

Being old is only good if you are an inanimate object. Simply look at all the antiques in those glossy antique books and note the prices they command. Then there are other things. Like Clyde Barrow's shirt. Not long ago a casino paid $85,000.00 for the bullet-ridden shirt that Clyde was wearing that day when he and his partner-in-crime, Bonnie Parker, took the wrong fork in the road. Probably when Clyde acquired the shirt back in 1933 it was considered an extravagance at $1.29. Imagine the following dialogue:

Clyde: "See my new shirt, Bonnie? Only $1.29."

Bonnie: "I can't believe you paid $1.29 for that excuse-for-textile. It's not even your colour. You're a winter, Clyde."

Clyde: "But, Bon, honey, it's not like I bought this with *my* money. I used some from the last bank holdup."

Bonnie: "Tut. Tut. *Whose* money?"

Clyde: O.K. O.K. *Our* money."

Bonnie: You're darn tootin' Clyde, baby. I had to dodge bullets just like you. And up in Missouri I snapped the elastic in my underwear grabbing on to that car door as you were driving away. Just remember, I'm an equal partner in this relationship."

Clyde: Well, gee, Bon. You don't have to get so fired up over one little word. After all, don't you get first billing on all the wanted posters and on the radio broadcasts? It's always 'Bonnie and Clyde, Bonnie and Clyde.' Just one time why can't it be, 'Clyde and Bonnie?'"

Bonnie: "Probably because B comes before C. Anyway, 'Bonnie and Clyde' flows better. I'm a poet. I can understand that. You can rhyme more words with 'Clyde' - like: 'hide, snide, lied, died...' "

Clyde: "Well anyway, I saw the shirt, I liked it and I bought it. There's no need to jump all over me. When you buy something new do I ever say anything?"

Bonnie: "When do I ever buy anything new?"

Clyde: "What about that long green skirt you wore to that holdup over in Arkansas?"

Bonnie: "*That* old thing? I've had that for ages."

Clyde: "I'll bet."

Bonnie: "What did you say?"

Clyde: "Nothing. Just thinking out loud, how someday maybe this shirt might be worth a lot of money."

If Clyde had known then just how much the shirt would bring and the fate it would meet, he would probably have had it Scotchguarded.

It's not only shirts belonging to notorious criminals that command big bucks. It can be something as innocent as a child's teddy bear. In particular, a 90-year-old teddy that belonged to the late King Frederick of Copenhagen. At one of those auctions for the rich and famous, this yellow bear with a red scarf around its neck brought $43,000.00. Someone found it in the attic of a royal castle, immersed in Styrofoam chips and stuffed inside the box that had contained the VCR. The box was sealed with duct tape, which is why no one had opened it for almost ninety years. Actually, I'm kidding. The bear was really found in a box marked, "Inkjet Printer," along with a three-year extended warranty from a discount electronics store.

With all of this in mind, take a look around your home or office and survey your worldly goods. Will any of them ever command the fortunes of Clyde Barrow's shirt or King Frederick's teddy? Perhaps the miniature Gumby and Pokey? That green felt skirt with the white poodle on the front? The original Chet Atkins guitar book, complete with Chet Atkins? Somehow I doubt it. None of those will ever be considered noteworthy or notorious. So even though you may own a few Beanie Babies and a Cabbage Patch doll, those items probably have no royal connections. Face it, if you are one who reads the daily paper in a t-shirt with a logo that announces: "I don't do mornings!" there is no lasting glory, only today. You may as well pour another cup of coffee.

THE PYSCHOLOGICAL RAMIFICATIONS
OF PROFESSIONAL ENCOUNTERS

There are three people in your life who will make you feel old: your doctor, your dentist and your ophthalmologist. A visit to any one of these will precipitate an appointment with a lawyer to get your affairs in order.

The doctor: It appears at first glance that doctors are getting younger. But part of that may be due to the fact that you have aged significantly while waiting for your appointment. Not only do you lose three hours of precious existence while sitting in the waiting room, another two hours is lost in the actual office itself, where you wait for the doctor to attend to five other people who were booked for the same appointed time. This is not so bad if you have remembered to bring a copy of *War And Peace* along. Actually, it is probably the only way you will ever get to read *War And Peace* in its entirety.

There is another thing that doctors do to make you think they are much younger than you are. They're always saying things to make you FEEL older. Things like, "You're not as young as you used to be, you know." or "You really have to slow down." or, that "mother of all" debilitating pronouncements that begins with "At your age..." It's a technique they learn in medical school and they become very good at it.

The dentist: This is the person who holds a licence to terrorize, torture and mutilate and then charge you for it. Somehow we have been led to believe that this is good for us and if we object too strenuously the dentist has a clincher that he or she delivers in two little words: "gum disease." This works better than the concept of hell described in The Book of Revelation. *Whosoever does not keep regular dental appointments shall suffer gum disease.* Dentists and doctors learn the same dialogue. Yours may utter something like, "It looks like you've had these fillings a LONG time." But it is merely a ploy, an excuse for him to extract every scrap of metal in your mouth and then extract enough from your bank account to send his first born to medical school. Dentists not only make you feel OLD; they also make you feel POOR. **The ophthalmologist:** This is the person who enters the personal space you only allow to intimate friends, close family members and lovers. They slide up to you in a minty aura of breath freshener and blow air into your eye. Actually, it's pepper spray. Then they make you read a chart: "Run Dick run. See Spot." When you realize how long it has been since you read those words in primary school, you are feeling older than King Tut's class ring.

During one visit to my ophthalmologist I pointed out a tiny growth on my lower eyelid. He glided into my personal space, took out his little penlight and examined my eye. Finally, after a prolonged examination, he rolled backward on his stool, flashed me a smug little smile and said, "You have an old chalazion (he pronounced it SE LAY ZHUN)." I bristled. "I already know THAT," I said, "now what is wrong with my EYE?" Not content with one insult, he launched another blow. "You know, the lens thickens with age," he said, his baby blue eyes sparkling like Austrian crystals. "So does the waistline," I answered, resisting the urge to poke him in his own personal space, the part that was stretching the imagination of his black leather belt.

Finally, with my dignity intact, I took my old chalazion and my thickened lenses and went next door to the drug store where I bought some 1.75-power reading glasses.

There's not a lot we can do to avoid visiting these harbingers of the inevitable. We can, however, take consolation in the knowledge that one day a doctor, dentist or ophthalmologist will tell them the same things they are presently telling us. When it all threatens to become too much for me I remember my 97-year-old great aunt. When her doctor asked her in that patronizing tone younger doctors use on the elderly, "Mrs. P., at your age, how do you put in the time?" she answered, "Oh, I just move a little slower."

99

MY BATTLE WITH ATW

In the spring of the year when the air is filled with the essence of hyacinth and lilac, the affliction returns: ATW - Addiction to Wallpaper.

I think it started when I was four years old, as I watched my mother perform wallpaper magic on the walls of our neighbours' homes. From that early age I loved the feel and smell of the wet paper and I ate enough wallpaper paste to hold me together for the rest of my life.

When I had been married about seven years, we purchased our first home - seven large rooms all crying for renovation. I marvelled at the instant transition that wallpaper created. Whenever I walked into a freshly papered room I felt all warm and toasty inside. Two years later, we moved to a bigger house - ten rooms and twelve-foot ceilings - just waiting for my personal touch. I discovered paper that looked like brick, linen, stone, and woodgrain, all of which were ideal for hiding structural defects and cracked plaster. I had teapots in the kitchen, rainbows in the bath, and the walls of my children's rooms were covered in kittens and airplanes. Flocked red paper gave the dining room a profound elegance and shiny gold paper in the living room provided a Victorian look.

I always papered alone; however, there were times when a travelling salesman came to the door, to be greeted by a little woman wrapped in a wallpaper sari. As my ATW intensified I knew I had to find someone who shared my obsession. I found Carol Anne. We spent hours together in wallpaper stores, planning our next project. I could phone Carol Anne and say, "Come over and see my newly papered bedroom" and know I would not be judged. And she felt no shame in confessing to me that she had "papered the bathroom with road maps last night at 10:00." One weekend when her husband went fishing he returned to find the walls of his den covered with ducks. "She even painted my wooden decoy a co-ordinating colour," he whined.

Our children became concerned. One day when her daughter was visiting I asked, "Why didn't your Mom come over too"? Her answer was one of resignation mixed with just a shade of disdain. "Oh, she's doing her little wallpaper thing again."

One day our seven-year-old son invited a friend over to play. Little Bobby, his mother a white-paint adherent, was fascinated by my wallpaper skills. Later on that afternoon my son came to me and said, "I can't find Bobby." There was a moment of panic as I glanced back along the wall I had just finished papering. Was it possible that Bobby ...? But no, we finally found him, in the bottom of a cupboard where he had fallen asleep. I guess he just felt all warm and toasty when he saw the papered interior.

All of that is history now. Several years ago my husband and I crossed the twin bridges of retirement and downsizing. The first time we walked into our white-walled condo with its panoramic ocean view, he whispered softly, "It's perfect - just the way it is." The subliminal message? No wallpaper, please.

For a while I held my penchant in check, being content to wander through wallpaper stores and simply fondle their wares. But one day, deep in withdrawal, I said to him, "Don't you think a nice nautical border would give more character to the dining room?" The slight nod, given before he could catch himself, was all I needed. I pulled out the border I had been hiding under the bed and two hours later he found himself surrounded by lighthouses and schooners in full sail. Encouraged now, I returned to the wallpaper store and purchased a border of large white magnolias which transformed the bathroom into a tropical delight. Next came a touch of dark blue paper behind the cupboards. Suddenly I was starting to feel all warm and toasty again.

In a desperate effort to ward off this imminent relapse of ATW, my husband suggested we buy a computer. I started composing newsletters. I found immense satisfaction in fitting all those little clip-art pictures and text frames together on a page. And then there's that wonderful "Cut" and "Paste" function. Who knows, perhaps when I have enough newsletters I can use them to paper the guest bathroom. Ah, already I'm feeling warm and toasty...

THE SCOTCHGUARD ASSAULT

It happens every spring. A young man with a face as fresh as a newly-hatched mayfly appears at the door, draped in two hundred metres of flexible hose and wearing a smile wide enough to cover the Canadian prairie.

"Hi, I'm Rick," he says, "and I'm here to shampoo your carpets."

I walk him through the house, pointing out areas that need special attention such as the tea stain beside my favourite chair, the grease spots in the entry where my husband swore he removed his boots, and the rosy blob shaped like Queen Elizabeth's profile - a souvenir of my last wine and cheese party. The young man nods and clucks, while the charm that drips from him calls for a "Caution! Wet floor" sign.

I always put this encounter off as long as possible, at least until my carpets assume an all-over smoky hue. It's not that I don't believe in cleanliness. On the contrary, I have been credited with a rise in stock prices for Mr. Clean and Lysol products. What wears me down during rug cleaning season is the Scotchguard solicitation.

I know, as we proceed down the hall and into the bedroom, that it's only a matter of time. However, from past experience I have learned not to mention Scotchguard early in the relationship. It's much better to keep them guessing - will she or won't she?

Finally I turn the house over to Rick and seek refuge in the kitchen on the pretext of cleaning cupboards. And I wait. This time, I promise myself, I will not submit, yield or bow to the Scotchguard assault.

An hour later Rick calls me into the living room where my newly cleaned carpet glows like a fresh snowfall under a full moon.

"Beautiful," I say as I follow him through the rest of the house. "How much do I owe you?" It's a superficial question. We both know I asked for the $69.00-three-room special advertised in the mail flyer.

And now it comes. Suddenly I am bombarded with 1001 reasons why I need to Scotchguard my rugs, the greatest of which is that they will "hold up" longer. According to Rick, if I subscribe to his treatment, I won't have to shampoo them for at least ten years. There is only one catch. This finishing school for rug cleaning costs $140.00, twice the price of the advertised special.

If Scotchguarding is so great, perhaps it should be implemented in other areas of our lives. Marriage, for example. Instead of exchanging rings, the couple could have the marriage commissioner or minister simply spray them with Scotchguard, assuring that their marriage will "hold up" for at least ten years. When I jokingly propose this to my young salesman, he is not amused. I have interrupted his practiced preamble. His brow is starting to ripple the way the ocean does when the breeze picks up.

I try another tack. "I was just reading in the newspaper where $8,000.00 to $10,000.00 every year is set aside for general maintenance of Stornoway, the home of the official Opposition leader in Ottawa. (I add this last part because I think the young man may believe that the official Opposition is me.) I plod on, watching his face as it slowly dissolves into confusion. "Apparently this general maintenance is 'cleaning carpets and checking the furnace.' Since a furnace check costs about $100.00, that means that approximately $9,900.00 is spent on carpet cleaning. Supposing there are upwards of twenty rooms in Stornoway that need attention, and supposing the leader of the Opposition asks for cleaning specials, I figure it can't cost more than $500.00 to shampoo all the rugs in the entire place, which means that $9,400.00 must be spent on Scotchguarding. Perhaps your company should look into doing the carpets there. Or maybe they could spray the leader of the Opposition with Scotchguard and guarantee he would be around for ten years but - wait a minute - it appears that has already been done."

I have elaborated too long. Somewhere along the way, my young salesman has retrieved his original train of thought. Regaining some of his former composure, he launches into another assault, more animated this time, and suddenly I am having what Yogi Berra once described as, "deja vu all over again." I am in a discount electronics store, face-to-face with a charming young zealot who is trying to sell me an extended warranty for our new television. He doesn't even flinch when I ask, "If the television is as good as you say it is, why do I need an extended warranty to ensure that it will do what you assured me it would do when you sold it to me?" His charm is forming in little puddles around his feet.

"Well, ma'am, your grandchildren might spill something on your t.v."

I tell him all my grandchildren live six hundred miles away and their parents are too financially challenged to pay me a visit.

"You might have a party and one of your guests could spill wine on the television," he persists.

I tell him my guests only spill wine on my CARPET.

"In five or six years your colour might fade. Under the warranty we will come to your house and re-adjust it at no cost to you."

All of this is running through my mind as I sit down to write a cheque to young Rick while he wraps 200 metres of flexible hose around his neck - $69.00 plus $140.00 equals $209.00 plus GST. Yes, I promise myself as my colour begins to fade, next time I will be more prepared. Next time I will not falter. I will not fail.

Finally I have the house to myself. I slump down in my favourite chair and flip on the television. As I make a mental note to call the electronics shop to send someone to adjust the colour, I formulate a plan. From now on I will rent a shampoo machine for my rugs and buy a can of Scotchguard to spray the television.

WHEN THERE'S GLOBAL WARMING, WHO NEEDS FLANNEL?

There I was at the breakfast table, drinking coffee and reading *Dear Abby* when I had my first hot flash. It was time to embrace that female rite of passage I had heard about, read about, and wondered about for years. I decided that a scientific approach was the best one. Obviously the best way to begin any scientific research project is with a professional definition. *Webster's Dictionary* summed it up nicely:

hot flash - "a sudden brief flushing and sensation of heat caused by dilation of skin capillaries usually associated with menopausal endocrine imbalance." So far, so good.

Now I needed a research partner, preferably someone of the opposite sex who could maintain complete objectivity. The obvious choice was the man with a science degree sitting on the other side of the table - my husband.

I stopped reading Abby's advice to "Fed Up in Michigan." I had to. I needed the *Life* section of the newspaper for a fan. As I began to calculate how much heat can be generated by a female Homo sapien in a state of nuclear meltdown, I asked my research partner for some scientific confirmation, "Do I look hot to you?" He looked up from his plate of bacon and eggs, surveyed me for a few seconds, and said, "You look fine," then went back to the business of eating.

I pondered the scientific designation of "fine." Does it lie somewhere between "hot" and "normal?" Does "fine" mean appearing "cool" even though the blood surging through your veins has reached the melting point of lead?

Responsible scientific investigation requires a second opinion. I decided to consult my sister. Even though my sister has never attended university, she has a great deal of technical knowledge, having passed through her menopausal period eight years ago. Therefore, when we got together for lunch a few days later and my capillaries had dilated to the width of the St Lawrence River, I asked her the same scientific question, "Do I look hot to you?" She pulled down her reading glasses, keeping her finger on the *Lite Fare for Seniors* section of the menu, and studied me for some time. Finally she said, "You look fine," and went back to reading the menu. I have known my sister a long time. I had to take her word for it.

I decided to take my scientific research into the world of nutrition to see if there was a correlation between hot flashes and food. It appeared that one cup of coffee created a metabolic power surge strong enough to illuminate the entire city of Calgary. A glass of red wine and my endocrine system turned into a catapult, launching my internal body temperature higher than the ozone layer. From then on, any consumption of coffee or red wine was left to my alert research partner who continued to maintain that I looked "fine." A good friend suggested the use of soy in my diet. Over the next few weeks I consumed enough soy products to raise the standard of living of every soybean farmer in North America. My research partner, to keep his mental faculties acute, ate steak.

At times this menopausal experience took on shades of spiritualism. I often had a sense of deja vu - of living back home with my parents in the wintertime - my mother turning the thermostat up and my father turning it down. At other times it was an image of my grandmother, her feet immersed in a bucket of cold water, fanning herself with a copy of *Farmer's Almanac*. Only now *I* was the one with the fan - the latest issue of *Seniors Alive*.

Since everything I read about menopause advised an exercise program, I joined a gym. It certainly had its benefits; mainly the view - hard, muscular, sweat-drenched bodies belonging to young Homo sapien males. One day, while hefting two five-pound barbells in front of the wall mirror, I noticed my face was the colour of an ocean sunrise. As I put the barbells back in their place, the gym assistant assured me I was doing "fine."

Then there were the night sweats. It was like a dip into hot tar, without the feathers. Pyjamas and nightgowns regularly went sailing through the dark like silently-launched V2 Rockets. This was a behaviour my research partner could never understand. For my September birthday he bought me a cute flannel night gown with long sleeves and a lace-trimmed collar - the perfect gift for a bed partner who, for the past thirty years, had maintained a night time body temperature of two degrees above absolute zero. As soon as I slipped it on, I threatened to self-incinerate. Rolling up the sleeves was no help. Who needs sleeves? Who needs a collar? Who needs a night gown? All of this appeared to be lost on my research partner who whispered that I looked "fine."

Scientific investigation requires two things: precise journalizing and graphs. On the back of the hydro bill I sketched a graph to follow the intensity and frequency of my hot flashes for twenty-four hours. The resultant black line resembled one for the Dow Jones on a good week of trading. In my scientific journal I scribbled the following hypothesis: "Hot flashes have their own intelligence. They come as often as they wish and stay as long as they like."

Now, ten years later, my research into "dilation of skin capillaries associated with menopausal endocrine imbalance" has ended. The conclusion recorded in my scientific journal is encapsulated in thirteen words: "Hot flashes are merely speed bumps on the road of a woman's life." I realize that, despite all of my efforts, I haven't shed any new light on the subject of menopause; however, I think I just might have stumbled upon the scientific discovery of the century. It concerns global warming. Scientists tell us that global warming is the result of the build-up of greenhouse gases caused by burning fossil fuels. Not so. The real reason for the greenhouse effect is the build-up of heat being generated by fifty million Baby Boomer females on the North American continent who are entering menopause. Which means, in another decade or so, it will turn cold again. Maybe then I will pull out that cute flannel nightgown.

www.ingramcontent.com/pod-product-compliance
Lightning Source LLC
Chambersburg PA
CBHW062004040426
42447CB00010B/1899